Philip Bennett Power

The Feet of Jesus in Life, Death, Resurrection and Glory

Philip Bennett Power

The Feet of Jesus in Life, Death, Resurrection and Glory

ISBN/EAN: 9783741188596

Manufactured in Europe, USA, Canada, Australia, Japa

Cover: Foto ©Lupo / pixelio.de

Manufactured and distributed by brebook publishing software (www.brebook.com)

Philip Bennett Power

The Feet of Jesus in Life, Death, Resurrection and Glory

THE FEET OF JESUS

IN

Life, Death, Resurrection, and Glory.

BY

REV. PHILIP BENNETT POWER, M.A.,
FORMERLY INCUMBENT OF CHRIST CHURCH, WORTHING.
AUTHOR OF "THE 'I WILLS' OF THE PSALMS," ETC.

LONDON:
HAMILTON, ADAMS, & CO., 32 PATERNOSTER ROW.
1872.

THESE PAGES ARE DEDICATED

BY THE AUTHOR,

TO THE MEMORY OF TWO MEN,

WHO "SERVED THEIR GENERATION BY THE WILL OF GOD,"

THE ONE,

The Rev. Edmund Clay, M.A.,

LATE INCUMBENT OF ST. MARGARET'S CHAPEL, BRIGHTON:

THE OTHER,

Charles Brook, Esq.,

OF ENDERBY HALL, LEICESTERSHIRE,

EACH FAITHFUL TO THE PARTICULAR TALENTS

COMMITTED TO HIM;

BOTH LEAVING AN EXAMPLE, WELL TO BE IMITATED,

HARD TO BE EXCELLED.

CONTENTS.

I.

THE FEET OF JESUS THE PLACE FOR HELPLESS MISERY.

"And great multitudes came unto Him, having with them those that were lame, blind, dumb, maimed, and many others, and cast them down at Jesus' feet; and He healed them."—MATT. xv, 30.

Even one footprint of Jesus beyond man's understanding—Christ's feet the place for helpless misery—Christ the centre of a circle of misery with an undefined circumference—Beauty of indefiniteness of "many others"—Why Christ is the centre of the circle of misery—Christ an ingatherer of human misery—Contrast of Christ's healing and that of the pool of Bethseda—Christ cannot but heal—Conscious helplessness has a power with Jesus—The power of just lying at the feet of Jesus—The power of simplicity in trust and pity—The cross, and the one who hung upon the cross—Our stricken ones to be brought to the cross .... Pages 1—10

II.

THE FEET OF JESUS THE PLACE FOR PERSONAL MINISTRATION.

"And, behold, a woman in the city, which was a sinner, when she knew that Jesus sat at meat in the Pharisee's house, brought an alabaster box of ointment, And stood at His feet behind Him weeping, and began to wash His feet with tears, and did wipe them with the hairs of her head, and kissed His feet, and anointed them with the ointment."—LUKE vii, 37, 38.

Man's probable idea of the revelation of the Son of God—Necessity for Christ's appearance in abasement, from our human nature, for belief in His sympathy, for offering sympathy ourselves—God's embodiment of thoughts of beauty—His will that we should do the same—The activities of practical Christian life constructed, based upon, and energized by the personality of Jesus—The cumulative service of the washer of feet—The services of "law" and "love"—Recognition of the component parts of service—Comfort for those who cannot aim high in service—The wiping and washing—The tear and the hair—Quality, not quantity, in service—The service of the person before that of the substance—The ministry of the kiss—Happiness amid tears—The power of the feet of Jesus to absorb service—Small spheres—What to do with our tears .... Pages 11—22

III.
THE FEET OF JESUS THE PLACE FOR PERSONAL NECESSITY.
(JAIRUS AT THE FEET.)

"And, behold, there came a man named Jairus, and he was a ruler of the synagogue: and he fell down at Jesus' feet, and besought Him that He would come into his house."—LUKE viii, 41.

"For a certain woman, whose young daughter had an unclean spirit, heard of Him, and came and fell at His feet."—MARK vii, 25.

"Then when Mary was come where Jesus was, and saw Him, she fell down at His feet, saying unto Him, Lord, if thou hadst been here, my brother had not died."—JOHN xi, 32.

The need of numbers, of individuals—The power of personalities in the Bible—Misery analyzed by God and Christ—The threefold sorrow of Jairus—Mingled sorrow—Concentrated sorrow—Comprehensive sorrow—The sorrow of Jairus—Misuse of the word "misery"—Jairus as the "ruler" as well as the "father"—The ruler at the feet—Circumstantiality in the detail of sorrow .... Pages 23—33

IV.
THE FEET OF JESUS THE PLACE FOR PERSONAL NECESSITY.
(THE SYROPHŒNICIAN WOMAN AT THE FEET.)

"A certain woman, whose young daughter had an unclean spirit, heard of Him, and came and fell at His feet: the woman was a Greek, a Syrophœnician by nation; and she besought Him that He would cast forth the devil out of her daughter."—MARK vii, 25, 26.

The Syrophœnician woman brought to the feet of Jesus—Preliminaries to coming to the feet of Jesus—These in the case of the Syrophœnician woman—The need of being *placed* for certain blessings—Mistakes as to finality in any dealings—Christ's views for us deeper than our own—The Syrophœnician woman brought to the feet by apparent neglect—The woman remaining, arguing, enduring, persevering, and conquering—Difficulty of simply remaining—The power of quiet energy—Arguing permitted at the feet—The introduction of misery to the feet—Diverse treatments for diverse persons—Arguings and soul strivings carried on at the feet of Jesus—Emptying before filling—Foundation and skill of the Syrophœnician woman's argument—Low positions, if assigned, to be taken up—Much to be sought for even when under deep consciousness of demerit—Need, not to overwhelm—The Syrophœnician woman's three grounds of argument—The valley of Achor—Value of an eye for encouragement—The prize flower—Faith in possibilities—"Little dogs," comfort in the term—The endurance of apparent repulse—Spurning at the feet of Jesus—Dealings of unmingled brightness not always to be expected at the feet of Jesus—Great blessings consistent with personal withdrawals—Withdrawals rightly interpreted are on-leadings—Mercy for those whom we think outside the circle of blessing .... Pages 34—53

V.

THE FEET OF JESUS THE PLACE FOR PERSONAL NECESSITY.

(MARY AT THE FEET.)

"Then when Mary was come where Jesus was, and saw Him, she fell down at His feet, saying unto Him, Lord, if Thou hadst been here, my brother had not died.—JOHN xi, 32.

The agitated lake an image of our lives—The agitation of Mary—Mary's falling at Jesus' feet—The impotence of many; the omnipotence of the One—The impotence of human sympathy—Benefit of having a well-known Christ in the time of sorrow—Much can be dispensed with if we have Christ Himself—Those who do not know our connection with Jesus do not know our resources—The calm Mary in haste—The mingling of human feeling and spiritual sensibility—The contemplative not to raise us above human joy or sorrow—The emotion of Jesus joined to that of Mary—The speed of Mary's going forth, her leaving the many for the One—Mary's saying at the feet of Jesus—The use of the same words both by Martha and Mary—The two "*my's*"—"Our" and "my"—The "our" of Jesus—The confidence in Jesus—Love's true thoughts sometimes only surface ones—Want of confidence worse than ignorance—The "ifs" of life—"If" and "But"—The vicissitudes of spiritual life—Human feeling crowding out faith—The poverty of what we can bring to the feet—Benefit to others of our woes ....Pages 54—73

VI.

THE FEET OF JESUS THE PLACE FOR PERSONAL NECESSITY.

(MARY AT JESUS' FEET)

"And she had a sister called Mary, which also sat at Jesus' feet, and heard His word."—LUKE X, 39.

Variety in the word of God—Variety in the subject of "the Feet of Jesus"—Mistaken views of Martha—Christ's reception into Mary's house—The houses of the friends of Jesus—The reception of Jesus according to man—Giving to Jesus not equal to receiving from Him—The secret of Martha's mistake—Teaching from the sisterhood of Martha and Mary—Different degrees of attainment in the two sisters—Mary's position—Sentimental affection to Christ—The real activity of Mary—Mary's knowledge of the inner mind of Christ—"Giving," a necessity of Christ's life—Mary's position attacked by Martha—The nature of that attack—Attempts to make a partizan of Christ—Christ's defence of Mary's position discriminating and decided—Jesus' knowledge of the caring and troubled ones—Christ our refuge from restless people—Ditto from circumstances—Mary as jealous of the honour of the house as Martha—Archbishop Leighton on the gift of ourselves to God—Encouragement to those who have little to give—Jesus Himself mistaken and misjudged—Jesus in vindicating Mary forgetful of mere "self"—Truths rather than ourselves to be vindicated—Encouragement to invite Christ in our poverty—Christ's recognition of the worth of that which is communicable from Himself—We are to act on that knowledge—We are not to stop at thoughts of our poverty—Christ's visibly bearing that He should be left unserved .... Pages 74—97

VII.

THE DEMONIAC.

Part I.

(HOW THE DEMONIAC CAME TO BE AT THE FEET OF JESUS.)

"Then they went out to see what was done; and came to Jesus, and found the man, out of whom the devils were departed, sitting at the feet of Jesus, clothed, and in his right mind: and they were afraid."—LUKE viii, 35.

Perfect picture of light and shade in the history of the demoniac—The background of this picture—Preliminaries to the demoniac's coming to the feet of Jesus—Profound darkness of the demoniac—Libels of the heart—Dark thoughts about Christ Himself—The passive resistance of opinion issuing in the active one of effort—The heart's real voice heard by Christ—The resistance of debased intelligence—Foundation of all rejection of Christ—The standpoint of the demoniac—That of Christ—A common point between the demoniac and Christ—The fulness of Christ's manhood to be held fast—Our standing as men before the man Christ Jesus—The demoniac saved by what was in the man Christ Jesus—The "often" of the demoniac—our "oftens" ... Pages 98—109

VIII.

THE DEMONIAC.

Part II.

(THE DEMONIAC SITTING AT THE FEET OF JESUS.)

Great wants often make inadequate impressions—Variety of aspects in which the demoniac might be surveyed—The contrast of a completed cure—All approaches to Christ precious—External and internal change of demoniac—The reception of the demoniac into the fellowship of intelligent manhood—The demoniac the recipient of charitable kindness—Christ's drawing His people into fellowship of work—Many necessities left after the first work of grace—Inward and outward change—The destiny of the demoniac—The world given something to see in the believer—The Gadarene's recognition of the work done on the demoniac—The Christian's secrets with Christ—The demoniac a resting man—The calm enjoyment of divine life—Rest and unrest - The triumph of the immaterial over the material—Weihe's magic hand—The 'inward' in man—Dr. Tholuck and the young man—New born souls not to be hurried—Sensations and feelings not to be hurriedly shaped—The demoniac a satisfied man—The bad part ended for ever—The future, not to trouble us with fears—Matamoros, and his fellow prisoner .... Pages 110—133

IX.

THE DEMONIAC.

Part III.

(THE MAN AS SEEN AT THE FEET OF JESUS.)

The Demoniac as seen by his fellow-countrymen at the feet—Men slow to perceive the visible advantage of the working of Christ—The power of material interest to hinder enquiry—Loss from lack of spiritual discernment—Intruding swine—Arguments for ourselves from Christ's gracious dealings.

Pages 134—139

X.

THE DEMONIAC.

Part IV.

(THE MAN AS SENT AWAY FROM THE FEET OF JESUS.)

The Gadarenes taken at their word—Probable thoughts of the demoniac—Probable motives—The demoniac's purpose for himself—Self-made purposes—" Away from the feet;" our thoughts on such a command—No lack of tenderness in the command—Our clingings to the material—Degraded and refined forms of the material—Christ's denial not unappreciative—A high commission given to the demoniac—Christ's recognition of earthly relationships—Ministry at home—Consecration of the highest instincts of humanity—Changed relationship to unchanged circumstances—" Spheres" and "ordered spheres"—Lone testimony—Judas and the demoniac .... Pages 140—152

XI.

THE FEET OF JESUS THE PLACE OF PERSONAL SUFFERING.

" They pierced my hands and my feet."—PSA. xxii, 16.

Various translations of the verse—The lions about the feet of Christ—The picture of Christ in pain—The profound mystery of pain—Geological testimony to pain—The first promise connects Christ with pain—Lazarus and the blind man—Great dignity in suffering—The feet as the means of escape—The means cut off—Christ's willingly taking up a position of helplessness—Enforced and accepted suffering—Jesus, as helpless, a representative man—The humbling condition of helplessness—Peculiar elements of trial in the helplessness upon the cross—A morbid glorying in being misunderstood—Christ's endurance of being misunderstood—His veiling of power—Christ's subordination of all to a purpose—The power of purpose in Christ—Christ hanging helplessly, a man of power—Christ's people partakers of His experience—The nobility of Christ's helplessness—The piercing a *part* of a great accomplishment—Our piercings not final—Only a part

of a great whole—Connection of the cross with our daily life—
The position of Christ's feet in relation to His enemies—The
mission of the pierced feet, as such—The pierced feet present
a view of the perfection of the suffering of Christ—Experimental sympathy of Christ ....Pages 153—173

THE FEET WHICH HAD GONE ABOUT DOING GOOD.

The ingratitude, folly, and madness of piercing the feet which had
gone about doing good—Injury endured in even the instruments of blessing—Why the goodness of Jesus did not protect Him—Correctives to foolish hopes of exemption—Jesus
in the Sanctuary of God, when dark thoughts were projected
on His heart—Loss, oftentimes but the mystery of a higher
call—The pierced feet traversing the world—The deeper will
of the Father—The pierced feet of Jesus entering on higher
service—The piercing, the end of suffering, the attainment of
rest .... Page 174—182

THE FEET WHICH HAD BEEN LOVINGLY TENDED.

No cups of bitterness without some sweet—This forms the bitter
element in 'contrast,' and did so to Christ—Job, and the
builders of the first temple—The power of 'contrast' working on Jesus—Jesus sowing contrast to reap contrast—We
are to meet contrast with contrast—The sobering power of
contrast—We are to minister while we can—The present, the
time for ministry—In all times of changes, the cross is our
resource .... Pages 182—195

XII

THE ANGELS SITTING AT THE HEAD AND FEET OF THE PLACE WHERE THE BODY OF JESUS HAD LAIN.

"*And as she wept, she stooped down, and looked into the sepulchre, and seeth two angels in white sitting, the one at the head, and the other at the feet, where the body of Jesus had lain.*"—JOHN xx, 12.

The Angels present at the death of Christ as well as at His birth;
at His grave, and in it—The presence of the Angels in the
tomb, a mystery—The actual body of Christ of supreme
importance—The helplessness of the dead body of Christ

very comforting to us—The incidents of Christ's helplessness to be brought into the incidents of ours—Heaven not ended with the dead body of Jesus—God always true to His own great plan—Invisible agents of attack met by invisible agents of defence—Luther and Melancthon hearing the children praying—The man with the book in Paradise court—The invisible instinct with holy influences for us—The special witness given to a loving one—Our great care for the body makes us forget God's—How to think of our dead in Christ
Pages 196—209

HONOUR FROM HEAVEN FOR THE WHOLE REJECTED ONE.

The tomb of Christ double sided—Rejection and reception bound together in it—The fulness of the witness to Christ in the tomb—The power of living with a concentrated thought.
Pages 210—213

THE PRESENCE OF THE ANGELS AT THE FIRST AND AT THE SECOND BIRTH OF CHRIST.

The tomb of Christ as 'the beginning of life' worthy of having honour conferred on it—The possibilities wrapped up in the life of Christ—Our views of the grave to be moulded on those of the grave of Jesus—Jesus a homeless One at His first and second birth—Homelessness yet heaven at the two extreme points of Jesus' life—The grave, a lodging—Jesus' rising, amid friends from heaven .... Pages 214—218

THE ADDRESS OF THE ANGELS AT THE HEAD AND FEET WHERE THE BODY OF JESUS HAD LAIN.

Christ, Mary's peculiar treasure—The tenacity of Mary's love—Love, amid perplexities—The angels though assisting at deep mysteries, full of sympathy—High functions not to take away sympathy—The condescension and courtesy of heavenly beings—The method of Christ's address to Mary—Probable reason for it .... Pages 218—227

THE SPEECH OF JESUS SURPASSING THAT OF ANGELS.

The limitation of the address of the Angels—Its teaching for us—Mary gradually led up to a blissful revelation—Jesus meeting in the neighbourhood of the grave—The method of Jesus' revelation of Himself—The intense humanity and super-humanity of the revelation of Jesus—Christ's appeal to Mary's inward consciousness—The power of the simple pronunciation of Mary's name by Jesus .... Pages 227—237

THE SITTING POSTURE OF THE ANGELS AT THE HEAD AND FEET OF THE PLACE WHERE THE BODY OF JESUS HAD LAIN.

The calm performance of duty by the angels, after the departure of the body—Its lessons for ourselves—The angels reveal to us the principle of service on a heavenly rule—Our need of learning this—The Angel's work brought to them—Their sitting posture, a corrective to many of our ideas Pages 237—242

XIII.

THE FEET OF JESUS THE PLACE OF WORSHIP.

"And as they went to tell His disciples, behold, Jesus met them, saying, All hail. And they came and held Him by the feet, and worshipped Him. Then said Jesus unto them, Be not afraid: go tell My brethren that they go into Galilee, and there shall they see Me."—MATT. xxviii, 9, 10.

Mary prohibited to touch and others permitted—The prohibition to Mary to touch at first sight mysterious—Steir on the subject—Strange interpretations given to it—Dr. Hannah on Mary's not being allowed to touch—The reasons which prevented Mary's touch did not exist as regards the other women—The actings of Christ sometimes in apparently opposite directions—Always adaptation in them—Discrimination in the dealings of Christ—Rest not to be found in sentiment—The balance of the Christian life—Surprises in the spiritual life—Confirmations in the spiritual life .... Pages 243—256

XIV.

THE FEET OF JESUS THE PLACE OF COMFORT.

"And when He had thus spoken, He shewed them His hands and His feet."—LUKE xxiv, 40.

The Lord's offering Himself to the touch—The terror of the Disciples at the appearance of Jesus—Controversy as to the Lord's entering through the door—Controversy as to the nature of His spiritual body—Teaching from Christ's appearing in a miraculous way—Thoughts of practical comfort to ourselves—The calm one ministering out of Himself—Jesus ministering out of His personality to our fears—Our Lord's setting right of 'thought'—Christ's 'very self' our 'very own'—Jesús ever wills to be recognized as 'the crucified'—All future explanations of Christ connected with 'piercings' Pages 257—263

XV.

THE FEET OF JESUS THE PLACE OF MANIFESTED GLORY.

"And His feet like unto fine brass, as if they burned in a furnace."—Rev. i, 15.

The helpfulness of this vision, though only partially understood—The light not repellent but attractive—Provision for the manifestation of the unbroken humanity of Christ—This manifestation essential to our spiritual life—Dreamy thoughts of glory not the will of God—Part of our interest in heaven lies in Christ's manhood—Manhood, dear to God—Good effects of believing in our future manhood—Christ's appearance in glory shews what God wills for us—Holiness, after Christ's example to be shewn in human nature—The grand contrasts of hereafter—The Father's remembrance as to the Son—God's recognition of contrast—The cheerings of contrast—Their entrance into homely life—The manifestation in glory of a whole Christ—Mistakes from partial views—Sustainment of excellence in Christ—Completeness in Christian life—Christ to be served as 'all holy'—The Saints shall rejoice in heaven in a *whole* Christ—A whole Christ cannot be fully enjoyed now—'Intense longings,' to be satisfied hereafter—The exaltation of that which is most lowly—Christ's view of lowly things—Our failure in them—How we are to view them—The ennobling of lowly services—Nothing in Christ which can sympathize with evil—Christ, to take the whole of us—Spiritual sorrows from the withholding of part of self—God's ideal, real—Christ's perfection of holiness, not a subject for terror, but joy .... Pages 264—289

XVI.

THE FEET OF JESUS THE PLACE OF MANIFESTED POWER.

"And His feet like unto fine brass, as if they burned in a furnace."—Rev. i, 15.

No weakness in Christ's character—The two-fold relation of His strength—To *us*, and to the Evil One—The holiness of habit better than the holiness of effort—The way in which the holiness of Christ should act on us—Edward Irving on this—The way in which it is destined to act on Satan—The comfort of feeling he is a doomed enemy—How to deal with present evil—The Feet of Jesus bringing light into darkness—His foot-falls to be seen in the valley of the shadow of death .... Pages 290—302

XVII.

THE FEET OF JESUS THE PLACE OF STRENGTH.

"And when I saw Him, I fell at His feet as dead."—Rev. i, 17.

Whether many or one are concerned, Christ's actings are all love—The Apostle overwhelmed as one in the flesh—Relief from Christ by the manifestation of Himself—Awful effects on the wicked, of Christ's manifestation—Effects upon believers of special manifestations—Revelations too much for the flesh designedly given—No believer allowed to remain overwhelmed—Kindness shewn to those brought by any means to the feet—Diverse acquaintanceships with the feet made in diverse ways—Suitability of brightness as the last appearance of the feet—Value to the Apostle and to us of his being obliged to fall prostrate—John raised wholly by a personal act of Christ—These personal acts what we have to look to—John vivified for service—No slavish life to be led in the presence of Christ's glory—The glory of future service—The power of full consciousness in future service—The grace which dealt with John as he fell at Jesus' feet will deal with us in all overwhelmings
Pages 303—315

THE FEET OF JESUS.

CHAPTER I.

THE FEET OF JESUS THE PLACE FOR HELPLESS MISERY.

"And great multitudes came unto Him, having with them those that were lame, blind, dumb, maimed, and many others, and cast them down at Jesus' feet; and He healed them."—MATT. xv, 30.

THE head of Jesus was crowned with thorns on earth; it is crowned with glory in heaven: and in either aspect we feel that it is a subject far beyond our grasp. It moves our feelings, it excites our admiration, and we wonder and adore where we cannot understand.

But the feet of Jesus! those feet which were weary, which were dust-soiled, which moved about the common haunts of man; perhaps we think we understand more of them. It may be that we do "more," but not "all." We do not understand all about any one footprint which He left on earth. There are reasons why He went to this place and to that, and why He left it, far beyond our ken. Yes; take any one footprint; see in it the earth or the dust of a fallen world bearing the impress of the foot of the Son of God made man; how comes that footmark there? What is the very first origin of it? what is the full extent of its meaning? There is no human intellect which can reach to this.

There are in this matter hidden things which belong to God; but there are also things revealed, which belong to us and to our children—things which intertwine themselves with our present position, with our daily need, with Christ's relationship to us, and ours to Him. It is upon such we desire to dwell in these chapters. We feel that we need the Spirit's guidance, to teach us so much as the least thing about even 'the feet of Jesus.'

In this great gathering, of which St. Matthew here speaks, we have the feet of Christ presented to us as the place for helpless misery—the place of simple pity. This scene is an epitome of the history of our Lord. Multitudes of diseased are on one side—Himself, the solitary Healer, on the other; they are cast at Jesus' feet, and He healed them. The feet of Jesus was the place for all this helpless misery; there it found simple pity; and in that pity a supply for all its need.

When I see, then, all these people cast at the

Place for Helpless Misery.

feet of Jesus, and lying there, the thoughts which I have are these:—

1. I see Him the well-defined centre of a circle, with an undefined circumference. I am glad that we are not told exactly how many were healed, and that we have not a perfect catalogue of the diseases under which they were suffering. I like to think what a vast number that "many others" may include—to think that from north, south, east, west, the miserable people all came. So large is the circle of human misery that, no human mind can even imagine its outer limits. We think, perhaps, that we know a good deal of deep heart-sinkings and sorrows ourselves; but, ah! others have some far deeper than ours; they are exercised on subjects and in ways that we have not an idea of, and in the vast sweep of all this misery stands Jesus the Healer—His feet are in the centre.

"Many others" were cast down at His feet. There is great beauty and use in the indefiniteness of Scripture—"*Whosoever* will, let him take of the water of life freely;" "Come unto me, *all* ye that labour and are heavy laden." It is meant to bring to the feet of Jesus all people ever so far off—people who otherwise never would have imagined that they might venture. The feet of Jesus is the place for all helpless misery—yours and mine, and "many others'."

But, in the matter of Christ, it is above all

things necessary that everything should be very precise; therefore, "Come unto ME." Therefore the sick were cast at His very feet. Christ entered the circle of misery for a purpose—that He might draw the miserable to Him. He stands, He sits, He walks in it, that He may be near people. His holy feet are down in our earth-dust, that creeping, or lying helpless, or cast down almost in despair, we may be near some part of Him; and to be near any part of Jesus is to be near healing and life. That woman who touched the hem of His garment bent close to His foot, and even there found all that she required.

2. I think that Jesus is a gatherer in of human misery. It was to be such an in-gatherer that He came on earth—that was His one object; to fit Himself for that He became man at all, and lived, and died. And here, He was a man above men. What most desire is, to ingather gain—for that they live, for that too often toil until they die. They desire to throw off misery; it is troublesome and expensive, and perhaps distressing to them; and what they throw off, Jesus takes. If we, then, are miserable in any way, and know not whither to go, or on whom to lay our load, let us bethink ourselves quickly of the ingatherer of sorrows. Did not His feet travel, when on earth, to the abode of illness and of death? did they not stand still, when He was cried after? He never used those, His human feet, to run from misery, or like

the priest and Levite to pass by on the other side; but He stood, and walked in misery's way.

Now we must lay this to heart. When we are miserable we must not say, "Where shall I go for sympathy? who will pity me? who will understand me, or my sorrow, or my case?" Behold, the ingatherer of all human misery is walking close by you; there is no path of sorrow which does not bear an imprint of His foot.

3. I have also a thought concerning the pool of Bethesda. There, a multitude were waiting, and only one could be healed. There was no eye of sympathy to look upon the afflicted, no voice to speak to them; each man, forgetful of perhaps the greater woes of others, absorbed only in his own, rushed forward, if possible, to be the first into the troubled waters; and so reap the solitary blessing which the pool contained.

Here, on this mountain-side, sits Jesus. There is no troubling here; there need not be. Whatever troubling there is, is always on man's side. With Him all is calm. We see in our mind's eye the multitudes toiling up the mountain-side; the eagerness, the anxiety, the casting down at Jesus' feet; and beautifully simple is all that we have told us of what He did, "He healed them all." Those simple words, no doubt, fitly express the calm with which He wrought upon the mass of misery prostrate at His feet.

4. And I think that, in truth, there lay before

Jesus, if we might be bold enough to say so, no alternative but to heal them all.

The only alternative was to get up and go away; or tell the people who brought their loved sick ones, to take them back again unhealed; but what an alternative would that have been to *Him!* *He* could never have done this.

So, then, when we cast down our sorrows, or ourselves, or our friends' sorrows, or themselves, right at the feet of Christ, let us think, 'He cannot go away from them.' This is no presumption, no lowering of Jesus, no detraction from His power; but it is a holy faith and courage to have such a thought, and it is greatly honouring to Him. What would become of us, if it had been even once recorded that Jesus was too busy to attend to such and such a person, or that He refused any one, and sent him away unhealed? No doubt Satan would say, "Ah, that case is just like yours;" or our own poor mistrusting hearts would be sure to fix upon it, and to feel, "So and so was sent away; ah! my experience may be the same."

But Jesus, owing to the blessed pitifulness of His nature, cannot go on—no, not a single step, if a helpless, suffering being, willing to be healed, is cast in faith athwart His path. He is rooted and bound by misery. Such is His blessed human nature that, if He were obliged to spurn the miserable from His feet, or to go away from them, He would be miserable Himself.

In our sorrow, then, let us look at Christ tied and bound by the laws of His own loving nature; let us put the power of those laws against our own fears, and the repulsiveness of our sins; and faith will strengthen itself, and lay many people, and many sorrows at the feet of Jesus.

5. Further, I think of the helpless misery of that crowd cast down at Jesus' feet. Lying there, they suggest the thought that conscious helplessness has in itself power with Jesus. Coming so closely in the sacred narrative upon the impassioned entreaty of the Syro-Phœnician woman at the feet of Jesus (which has a lesson of its own,) it seems to have a special teaching. For many might say, "We cannot plead as she did." Diffident of their own earnestness and energy; and seeing how much was won by the Syro-Phœnician woman by the exercise of these qualities, they might say, "If Christ has to be so hardly entreated, then what can we hope to get—we who are feeble, who seem as though we are not wise enough to use arguments which can reach His head, or strong enough to utter cries which can pierce His heart?" We need only read on a little further; and behold the multitudes simply lying at His feet.

These sick people thus lying at Jesus' feet have a voice to us—their helplessness speaks to ours; it says, "Perhaps you cannot address arguments like the Syro-Phœnician woman to the head of Christ; or, it may be, are dull in pleading with the affections of His heart; then do not consider that all is over—that there is nothing for you; do not depress yourself with what you cannot do; think rather of what you can. You can lie before Jesus, where he must see you; you are very close to Him, when you are at His feet."

In common, everyday life, men are frequently losing gain which they might have had, while aiming at something higher which they cannot have; so is it in the spiritual life too. While aiming at what is much higher than we at present have capacity for, we miss what is within our reach.

We must not fret ourselves that we have not attained to this or that energy of spiritual life, and shut out the comfort of knowing that we have "something"—that we are at the Saviour's feet. Satan would hide from us that we are there; for he knows that none tarry long there in humble waiting, without being lifted up and given strength.

If the reader feel very helpless, let him not flee from this thought, but use it; and the way he is to use it is this. He is to stay still where he is—not to want to move at all—not to be restless; Jesus sees him, that is enough.

6. Now I think how beautifully simple everything is here; the few and unadorned words in which this great transaction is recorded lead us to thoughts of simplicity. There is simple trust on

the part of the afflicted people, and those who brought them; and simple pity on the part of Jesus.

Blessed be God for all the simplicity in the gospels; it is as little children we must receive the kingdom of heaven, and simple food suits the infancy of the soul—aye, and its ripe old age. For when many things have been learned about types and prophecies, and many speculations have been made, and systems of theology constructed, what does the soul fall back upon when in view of eternity, but just the simple truth of "Jesus dead, and alive again for us?" That was what made a prelate eminent in learning and controversy say, in extreme old age, and in his dying hours, "Don't talk to me of the cross, but of the One that hung upon the cross."

This was no distinction without a difference. The cross had clinging to it more of a complex creed. The One who hung upon it (though His hanging there involved the creed) was what the soul needed; there were the very feet, at which it could lie.

Let us say to ourselves and to others, What is needed for healing is not many thoughts, or high thoughts, about Jesus, or any intellectual knowledge about Him at all, but the plainest simplicity of trust; and it will be very helpful if we see that the like simplicity is in Him. Simple pity! that is what we are to look for from Jesus. We need not connect it with any theological thoughts; it is a pure uncompounded feeling; and where shall we see it exercised as on those who are cast at His feet?

Let us learn, then, the value of bringing our afflicted ones to the feet of Christ, feeling we can do no more than that. We have perhaps tried many physicians with them, and they are no better but rather the worse. Kindness has not melted them, punishment has not corrected them, discipline has not restrained them. We must now not "cast them off," but "cast them down" at the feet of Jesus. And having done this, we must not yield to desponding feelings of helplessness. We are now really nearer to being helped than ever we were before. We are now in the right place before Christ—in the right position—that of expectancy, with the right feelings—those of self-helplessness, and yet hope. Who knows how soon you will say, "We cast them down at Jesus' feet, and He healed them?"

CHAPTER II.

THE FEET OF JESUS THE PLACE FOR PERSONAL MINISTRATION.

"And, behold, a woman in the city, which was a sinner, when she knew that Jesus sat at meat in the Pharisee's house, brought an alabaster box of ointment, and stood at His feet behind Him weeping, and began to wash His feet with tears, and did wipe them with the hairs of her head, and kissed His feet, and anointed them with the ointment."—LUKE VII, 37, 38.

IF man had been informed by God that He was about to reveal His only Son to the world, and had been asked what form this revelation should take, there is little doubt what his answer would have been. He would have said, "As the Son of God, it is meet that He should appear in great glory; a throne must be His seat, legions of angels His attendants; the music of heaven must float around Him, the radiance of heaven beam from Him; the eye without shading should not be able to look upon Him; nor the knee without trembling to stand before Him."

But the ways of God are not as our ways, neither are His thoughts like ours; and so, before He gives us a revelation of His Son in glory, with a countenance shining as the sun in his strength, with a head glorious with many crowns, and feet like unto fine brass, as though they burned in a furnace, He presents Him to us with a visage marred more than any man's; with head unpillowed and with feet unwashed.

For this, so unexpected an appearance—so low an abasement of the Son of God, there must have been deep reasons in His Father's mind. Some of these we ourselves can see; and such divide themselves into two classes—those which belonged to His humiliation as necessary for the atonement; and those which have to do with us in our feeling and communion with God, and practical spiritual life—internally in our thoughts, externally in our acts.

How would it have been with us, if we had not seen Christ, as it were, from head to foot, as He is revealed to us in the history of His life on earth—in the very fulness of His human nature? We never could have gone out to Him in *our* human nature. We might have taken off our shoes and worshipped where His feet had trodden, for it was holy ground; but we could never have walked with Him; we should have considered what was essentially human in us too small to come into contact with what was essentially and wholly Divine—with what was so great. The confidings of our human nature would have been all pent in. We should have been frightened to go with many a tale which we can now tell without fear. But why is it thus now, when His last appearance, as given in the Revelation, is so grand? Because many thorns preceded the many crowns; and weariness and neglect were the portion of those feet, which having passed heaven's threshold in triumph, now burn like fine brass.

Nor could we have believed in Christ's sympathy as we do now; our dull hearts would not have been so assured of His feeling for us, unless we knew that He also had felt trials like our own.

Nor could we have offered sympathy, as in the person of His people we can now. What a wonderful thought this is! God in Christ desires human sympathies; He has so arranged that these sympathies are possible, that they can reach Him —that we may offer Him our feelings; and He has given us the privilege of solidifying our feelings. This poor woman's offering to the feet of Jesus— her tears and ointment, and that lowly ministry of her hair, became, so to speak, solidified; the Jesus who turned water into wine has made them shine with a resplendent light for His Church through many ages.

God loves to embody His thoughts; they are so embodied in countless forms of beauty around us. He embodied them pre-eminently in Christ, and He wills that we should embody our sympathies with Jesus. Therefore let us do as this woman did—let us not merely talk, and look, but do. He who sympathises practically with the lowly ones of Christ, or with the small and worrying troubles of even the smallest of His people, does so with His feet—they wash, they wipe, they anoint, they kiss.

The activities of practical Christian life are constructed and based upon, and energised by, the personality of Jesus. Everywhere we are met by "the man Christ Jesus." Mere dreams and sentiments take flight before a substantial Christ. If only we will see it, He is still in our midst. Take Him away, and our spiritual life will be divested of a central, moving figure—one whose life on earth, as well as whose glory in heaven, His Father means ever to be before us.

And so, we might go on with many other evils which would happen, if we had not as a Christ One who with human feet walked the same earth as we do, and whose feet were ministered to with such acceptance as we find here.

Thus keeping before us the person of Jesus, we also may in our measure realise the apostle's words—"That which we have seen with our eyes, which we have looked upon, and our hands have handled of the Word of life."

Let us do all things so personally to Christ—let us hear His voice saying so plainly, "Inasmuch as ye have done it unto one of the least of these my brethren, ye have done it unto me," that we may indeed be able to take up those words and say, "What we have seen, looked upon, handled of the Word of life."

A large subject is embraced here, but we shall confine ourselves to the Feet of Christ as the place of personal ministration.

Let us mark here the cumulative or heaped-up nature of this woman's service. There was washing, wiping, kissing, anointing. It is like a cluster of diamonds in a single ring, like many fruits on one bough.

And the first thought which strikes us concerning it is a sorrowful one; it is the difference between this woman's cumulative service, and the poor, and often grudging service, which we offer. We look upon service too often as under law—that we are commanded to do this and that; it becomes the fulfilment of law, and nothing more. And so it comes to pass that, much of our service becomes grudging or of necessity, and inquires not "how much can be given," but "what will be enough," "what will barely do." The hardness which belongs to law enters into this service; and like all our attempts at law-keeping, it falls short.

But this woman's service was under no law. She was not even under the unwritten law of hospitality; for it was not in her house that Jesus was. This service was the representative not of law, but love; and in love it found a motive power, which law never could have supplied.

Let us aim at cumulative service—to do much to Christ; for in doing it *for* Him, we do it *to* Him. And let us remember that this service will not be noted merely in the mass, God will separate it into its component parts. Each specific good thing will be noted. God will unwind the golden thread into its various strands; He will pass the ray beneath a prism, which will divide it into many hues.

We take things in the lump; our grossness, our want of memory, our imperfect power of perception, all conduce to this; but God is too exact not to note the parts which make up the whole.

If we pay a visit to the sick for His sake, He notes all the component parts of that visit—the cheery word we uttered, the tone in which it was spoken, the gentle touch of the sick one's hand, the patient silence while listening to complaints, the loving craft by which we sought to while away the afflicted one from himself. In our mind—it may be, in the sick one's mind—we paid a visit, and that was all; but God knows what there was in that visit, and He counts it all up, and records it even as He does the washing, wiping, kissing, and anointing here.

The feet of Jesus were the recipients of cumulative love service; and what encouragement is there here to those who are diffident about aiming high.

The feet, at least, are open to them; they may pour out all their fulness upon what is very lowly, yet belonging to Christ. The lowliest object may be the recipient of cumulative service. Jesus Himself took care to point this out when He said, "Inasmuch as ye have done it unto one of the least of these my brethren, ye have done it unto me."

There is also a certain perfection in this service which the reader is invited to observe. There was washing and wiping. This was no half—no unfinished service, but one altogether perfect in its kind. The wiping was the needed sequence of the washing; and it is forthcoming, and that with no diminution of love's intensity; there were tears wherewith to wash, there was hair wherewith to wipe.

One fact which strikes us here is, the continued strength or energy of this service; the ministry of the tears of her eyes is immediately followed by that of the hair of her head. Surely this woman's hair and tears have a voice for us. When we put our service by the side of hers we are reminded how often we diminish, how often we leave unfinished, how often we think we have done enough, when there plainly remains yet more to be done.

Some of the most beautiful services in God's eyes are probably so from their perfection and not their extent. God loves what is perfect in its kind. Its kind may be very lowly; He Himself has made a great many very lowly things—little flowers and insects which make no pretension to being otherwise than lowly; but when He had seen everything that He had made, He pronounced it to be "very good." Lowliness of position and perfection of kind may go together.

It is a sign of a perfect workman not to leave anything unfinished; and Love should be of all workers the most perfect.

But there was another element of perfection in this ministry to the feet of Jesus. She gave not only herself but hers—after washing, wiping, and kissing, all three as it were givings of her very self, she anointed with the ointment from the alabaster box.

There were three personal services—services of herself—*before* there was the giving of substance. The ointment was very precious, but it did not weigh down what had gone before.

It might be said, service can be recognised in the washing and wiping; but what service was there in the kissing? The answer is that, a kiss is a service of love—a performance of the lip on behalf of the heart; the heart feeling that it must do something to show its love, and the lip lending it its aid. This woman probably uttered not a word during all this process of love—let it not be considered a contradiction in terms that, her kiss was the voice of voiceless love.

From the position in which the mention of her

kissing Jesus' feet is found—midway between the two ministries of the washing and wiping, and the anointing, a thought arises with reference to our own personal feeling in service. It must needs have been that, that worshipping woman had herself some of the enjoyment of love's sweetness and refreshment when she kissed those feet of Jesus. It is no irreverence, but strictly within the probability of things, to believe that an ineffable sense of happiness passed through her, as she thus vented upon the honoured feet of Jesus her adoring love.

I accept with comfort the suggestion which hereon rises in my mind. I say, "There is to be happiness for the server in his service, as well as honour for the served one, in being served."

And, reader, seek to enjoy this privilege. Do not argue against yourself and say, "How can there be any happiness where there are tears?" Ah! some of the most delicately-shaded happiness is found amid tears. There are flowers which are obliged to hang down their heads by reason of the heavy showers, but their perfume has not gone.

Seek for personal happiness when rendering to Jesus personal service; seek for refreshment to your own soul, when refreshing His people—*i.e.*, Himself.

Let us bracket kissing and anointing together, as we did washing and wiping; the one was a true symbol, the other a costly and substantial reality of love. Kisses may be poor things like Orpah's, or deceitful like Judas'; but when the kiss and the fatted calf go together—the kiss and the ointment—there is no mistake; the first two are given freely to us, the second let us give in turn.

But let us return more immediately for a moment from this ministering woman to the feet which were ministered unto. All was lavished upon the least, as it were of Jesus—upon His feet.

How often we think that only the head, some great cause of Jesus, or enterprise for Him can be worthily served by our greatest; but we are thus underrating the least of His, overrating the greatest of ours.

The feet of Jesus had here a great capacity for absorbing service, the washing, wiping, kissing, anointing, were all accepted and appreciated.

We know that the very head of Jesus may be anointed—that He graciously places it within our reach; that what may be called great enterprises for Him may be undertaken; but for the most part we have to do with the feet.

Let not the reader, then, sigh after great spheres of service, or want great outvents for love to his Saviour. He that is untrue in the least would be also untrue in the greatest; he who neglects the feet would neglect the head. Amid the dust-soiled, the wayworn, and the neglected will be found recipients capable of absorbing all the service that we can give. Like the feet of Jesus, they lie within our reach; it is only meet that the lowest and the least of God's should be able to absorb the greatest and the best of ours. It will be a great encouragement to us in our ministerings amongst humble persons, or in doing humble offices, to remember that they actually have a capacity for swallowing up our utmost efforts—they are big enough for the most that we can do.

From amongst many others which lie to hand, let us just take one point more for a moment's thought.

What shall we do with our tears? The world is full of tears, and many of them are wasted. Now there should be no waste of anything, and tears are not intended to be spilt upon the ground. The Psalmist knew that God valued tears when he said, "Put my tears into thy bottle."

Tears are to be brought into connection with Jesus. The tears which touched the feet, thrilled through the being of the Lord. We may hold back, thinking that we cannot reach the heart of Christ; but let us touch Him anywhere, His whole being is sensitive, He will soon say, "Somebody, something has touched me."

And now, lastly, let those who read these lines make up for the neglect of duty by others, by the exuberance and fulness of their own love.

Simon's duty, in common hospitality, was to have

given Jesus water for His feet. He gave it not; but this woman supplied its place with tears.

May we have the love which will supply the deficiencies even of those who profess to entertain the Lord. The closest personal services done to Him—those which will gain most place in that history which is for eternity—are those, not of duty, but of love; and many of them done, as it were, only to the "feet of Jesus."

CHAPTER III.

THE FEET OF JESUS THE PLACE FOR PERSONAL NECESSITY.

(JAIRUS AT THE FEET.)

"And, behold, there came a man named Jairus, and he was a ruler of the synagogue: and he fell down at Jesus' feet, and besought Him that He would come into his house.—Luke viii, 41.

"For a certain woman, whose young daughter had an unclean spirit, heard of Him, and came and fell at His feet.—Mark vii, 25.

"Then when Mary was come where Jesus was, and saw Him, she fell down at His feet, saying unto Him, Lord, if Thou hadst been here, my brother had not died."—John xi, 32.

WE have in Holy Scripture something about the feet of Jesus, as regards His life on earth, His death, His resurrection life, and His life in glory. We are at present concerned only with incidents which refer to those feet, while He lived and moved as a man amongst men, in what we might call the ordinary walks of every-day human life.

No doubt, what meets us is very extraordinary, but the scenes in which we find it embrace the usual places, people, and things of daily life.

Amongst the various mentions which we find of Jesus' feet, that with which we commenced these chapters is the only one embracing numbers; all the rest have to do with persons—their individual feelings, their position, their need. And if we follow them out, we shall find them embodying and illustrating many of the experiences and feelings of Christian life. Here in the Syrophœnician, we see the trial and victory of Faith—Jesus allowing Himself to be overcome. In Mary after Lazarus' death, we find the venting of personal sorrow; in the Samaritan of gratitude. In the anointing woman we have seen personal love and ministry; in the woman sitting at His feet we have appreciation; in the man sitting, the recognition of the place of rest. The leper who fell down before Jesus gives us the expression of terrible personal need; and Peter at His knees, the abasement of felt personal demerit.

One great beauty of the Bible, and one of the means by which it takes such deep hold of us is, its personalities; our natures crave what is personal, and find it here; they fix upon it; they take special comfort from it.

We cannot take in the woe of masses; we have no capacity for doing so—it is well that we have not. A single case with all its particulars can be realized; we enter into it, and it affects us more than any amount of anguish, no matter how great, which is but a confused mass. We read of so many thousands being wounded in some dreadful war, but let there be in the article which states this, an incident of individual suffering, and the human mind instinctively fixes itself on that.

It is a blessed thought that all masses of misery resolve themselves into their component parts—into individual cases before God. The great mind is analytical—it goes into particulars and details.

And here—much of the soul's life—ay, and of the body's life too—might be said to be analysed at "the feet of Jesus."

Here we have the feet of Jesus the place for agonising personal suppliants—for the stating and pleading of individual need.

In the three cases, which we have grouped together at the head of this chapter, we might be said to have to do entirely with "death." In the case of the Syrophœnician woman, there was a living death—a life almost worse than death. In that of Jairus, there was present death—first threatened, then actual. In that of Mary, there was the finished woe; that dear body was dead—it was gone. As long as the body remains with us there is something to look at—something to be done—the mind feels there is something yet to come; but when that is taken away, there remains nothing more—

the woe is consummated—ah, me! it is well that there is such a place as the feet of Jesus.

In the first of our chapters we met with multitudes and passive misery; here we meet with single cases, where all is concentrated and active; and individual effort and energy are put forth in the highest degree.

We shall first consider the case of Jairus.

Here I find him—a ruler of the synagogue, at "the feet of Jesus!"

What brought him there? A threefold sorrow—a mingled, a concentrated, a comprehensive one.

It was mingled—the daughter's and his own; she lay a-dying; and forasmuch as his heart was bound up in hers, that heart might be said to be a-dying also.

Mingled sorrow might be said to be the higher sorrow; it is not purely selfish; it has to do with others' woe; it does not exclude 'self;' to be mingled, it must give 'self' its place; but it has to do with another also.

And this mingling is very close—here it is a father *for* an only daughter, and *because* of an only daughter; the two thoughts could be separated, but they are not meant to be so.

So is it with many of the sorrows which God appoints for us; our feelings for our dear ones and our own personal feelings are interwoven so as to become one.

But what we are principally concerned with here

is the fact that, this sorrow was brought to the feet of Jesus. And surely that was its appropriate place; because Jesus Himself was a man of mingled sorrows. He was not only a man of sorrow, but of sorrows—He tasted this kind as well as others; it is included under the head of His "acquaintance" with grief. The cup which the Father had given Him in Gethsemane was a mingled cup; those tears at the grave of Lazarus were mingled tears.

So, then, Jesus was the very one to whom a trouble like that of Jairus, or of the Syrophœnician woman, could be brought; His feet were their proper place.

And here let us bring our sorrows in their mingled form—let us not seek to scatter them; and look for comfort for one part here, and for another part there. Jesus, by His own experience, will understand the component parts of our grief.

And He will not be displeased because we seek relief for our own sorrow, as well as for the one on account of whom we are in grief. Personal sorrow is recognised; the same God who meant it to be felt, meant it also to be eased; and the place for ease by His appointment is the feet of Jesus.

I next note this as a concentrated sorrow—she for whom Jairus had come to the feet of Jesus was an only daughter. This sorrow, though mingled, was not diffused; it savoured much of an essence—an essence of woe. If the only daughter went, then all was gone. This woe was well defined indeed. And in this aspect of it, it found its fittest place at Jesus' feet. His own course of sorrow was well defined enough; He was continually coming into contact with facts, often in relation to His own closest disciples and friends, which grieved Him; He could have well-defined feeling for well-defined trial.

Let us remember this, for we are often thinking that our particular trial is infinitely more to us, than it is to Christ; that He does not see it to be as large as it really is; that He cannot feel it as we feel it, or understand it as we do; that His sympathies are so scattered and diffused, He cannot gather them into the focus of our one grief. Jesus can cause the rays of His sympathy to converge on one point, until He makes it glow and burn with a light and heat of love.

We must not fear, then, being intrusive, or say, "Why should I think that my sorrow which is so great to me, should be great to Him?" He will recognise it as being what it is to us. Even if it be an exaggerated sorrow—made so from our nervousness, still to us it is real, and therefore, it is so to Him.

An "only daughter;" here is a centre, a pivot, something around which the dried-up heart would grind in days and nights of sorrow.

And are there not some hearts which have unoiled centres of sorrow, around which they unceasingly grind? They perform the one dull round of grief—the eye so fixed on one central point, that it soon becomes incapable of taking in anything else. Let it be brought to the feet of Jesus, that is the only place for dealing with sorrow like this. Remember the picture painted for you here—it is that of one deep sufferer, about one sorrow, before one Helper.

We must glance at one more aspect of this sorrow. It was comprehensive. Like all, or almost all those connected with death, it took in a past and a future. Oh! the wide-spreading comprehensiveness of death—that circle with so sharp and well-defined a point for a centre, with so large and vast-embracing a sweep for a circumference.

Jairus brought a past to the feet of Jesus—a past full of endearment. For twelve years this child had been creeping around his heart, ever budding, ever throwing out fresh tendrils, which found their clinging place around that heart. For twelve years had she nestled inside it, so that his very life was as it were the enfolding of another. It may be that father with child, and child with father, they mingled their lives together. Perhaps, this only daughter had helped to keep this father fresh and young, by the sweet unconscious ministry of youth—for children minister to us by their toys, and laughter, and the fresh dew upon their early morning life; perhaps, he had often sat, and with sweet contentment watched the mother being reproduced in the child; who knows into what depths this "perhaps" will travel, if we let it go forth unrestricted into twelve years' life with an only child? It is said that fathers love their girls, and mothers their sons, the most; and whatever is that peculiarity of affection, it is beautiful to see how Jesus meets its sorrow, for He raised Jairus' only daughter; and the widow of Nain's only son. He not only gave them back their all, but a peculiar all; and, doubtless, He knew that He was doing so, for He is delicately skilled in the peculiarities of grief.

It was with such a past—a past with a great circle, and that, crowded with the imagery of love, that Jairus, the father, fell at Jesus' feet. But that was not all. He knows little of death-sorrow who imagines that it is all connected with the past. Far from it. The death-sorrow is a stand-point upon life's road with a past brightly peopled, with a future darkly blank.

I bear in mind the almost indignation with which a friend of mine—advanced in the life of faith, received a letter on her husband's death condoling with her on her "misery." To her, full of Christian hope, and well knowing that God had yet for her a life to be lived for Him, full also of all the consolations that the Gospel can give, the word was out of place—she felt it was a wrong to God; but consolations like these—certainly those high ones of the Gospel, this ruler had not; and so we may ponder how blank and void, how unseasoned and lustreless was that prospect which now lay before him.

The father had probably looked forward to much; he had day-dreamings of what that girl would be to him in his old age; a father's heart had often taken to love's speculations, and built castles in the air, which now lay ruined at his feet—ruined, not by slow decay of time, but, as it were, by a lightning flash. The girl was then a-dying—to all intents and purposes dead, unless Jesus would come at once and help; and Jairus embodying in himself these varied forms of sorrow —the mingled, the concentrated, and the comprehensive—fell with them all at Jesus' feet.

Up to the present, we have seen Jairus only as a father; but the narrative brings him before us in another character also—we are told he was "a ruler of the synagogue." And it is important to note this with reference to our present subject, "the feet of Jesus." A ruler of the synagogue, a great man, is before the One who was called the carpenter's son, and at His feet.

True need brings us very low. It brought down that ruler; it has done the same to many a one since. The rich, the honoured, the intellectual, have been brought there. They might have questioned with Jesus, and admired Him, and said, "Thou art a teacher come from God," and continued just as they were; but nothing, save a deep sense of need, would have brought them to the feet of Jesus.

All adventitious circumstances—all rank, riches, intellect, are swept away before the avalanche of urgent and tremendous need. Oh! how small these things seem in the presence of overwhelming need—especially when they come on the platform on which Death is already standing. That form makes an impertinence of them all. Our fancied personal importance becomes nothing there.

"A ruler" at Jesus' feet was a triumph of reality. And whither have we been brought, and what has "the real" done *for* us, or rather, *with* us? For there is a great difference between these two. Something must be done with us, before anything is done for us; we must be brought to the feet of Jesus, there to receive a life gift—a gift, which shall be a victory over death.

Let us take one more thought before we close this chapter.

When this ruler was at Jesus' feet he besought Him "that He would come into his house; for he had one only daughter, twelve years of age, and she lay a-dying."

The father invited Jesus to come into the very place, and scene, and home of sorrow. Into the place so lately instinct with joy, but which was now stilled; into the recesses of home life where everything which was associated with his departing joy lay around, there the ruler of the synagogue would bring Him who was in truth a higher ruler than himself, for He had power even over death.

We do not like the world or outsiders to see our deepest and most sacred sorrow, especially when it is fresh; but if our heart has apprehended Jesus aright, we shall be ready to ask *Him*. His will be no look of curiosity, no cold taking in of circumstances in which He has no interest; wherever He comes, whenever He speaks or looks, it is always with a purpose.

And let us be circumstantial in the detail of our sorrow. Jairus told the Lord that he had one only daughter, and that she was twelve years old, and that she lay a-dying. All that he said would be helpful towards exciting Jesus' interest and moving His pity; which perhaps, he, who knew not Jesus' heart fully, would have thought necessary. We know that for this purpose it is not needed; still it is a good thing to enter into particulars with the Lord. It is treating Him with confidence; the very feeling that He will be interested is honouring to Him. Every particular that we bring before Him, He will note; and act with reference to it too.

So then, when we analyse this sorrow of the ruler, we see that there was enough to bring him (ruler though he was) to the place where we find him here—the place for every reader of these lines, in all sorrowful times—" The Feet of Jesus."

CHAPTER IV.

THE FEET OF JESUS THE PLACE FOR PERSONAL NECESSITY.

(THE SYROPHŒNICIAN WOMAN AT THE FEET.)

"A certain woman, whose young daughter had an unclean spirit, heard of Him, and came and fell at His feet: the woman was a Greek, a Syrophœnician by nation; and she besought Him that He would cast forth the devil out of her daughter."—MARK VII, 25, 26.

THE first position which this woman took up does not appear to have been at the feet of Jesus. According to the account given us in St. Matthew, she seems to have followed Christ for some little time, probably at somewhat of a distance, crying after Him, and begging for mercy at once upon herself and her child. She was apparently within hearing distance, but that availed her nothing, for Jesus answered her not a word. And if she heard the answer which the Lord gave to the disciples, when they asked that she should be given what she wanted and sent away, her chances of help seemed about utterly to perish. But "the feet of Jesus" had yet to be tried. Neither had the mother's perseverance nor His grace been tested as yet to the uttermost; that saying, "I am not sent but unto the lost sheep of the house of Israel," which to some might have seemed a hurricane blast, enough to sweep her beyond all reach of hope for ever, was in truth intended to catch her in eddies, which swift circling would soon sweep her into the centre, and that centre was "the feet of Jesus."

Here, on the very threshold of the story, we are met by our first teaching. We have here one *brought* to the feet of Jesus. It may seem to us that, so as the mother's heart were eased and the afflicted child were healed, it would have been all one whether this were accomplished by speaking to the woman at a distance, or at the very feet; but we may rest assured it is not so. Whether we see it or no, there are reasons in all the diversities of circumstances attending each particular act of mercy.

And, first, let us observe that there are often preliminaries, and those not of a formal, but of a very important character, to our being found at the feet of Jesus. There are often preparations and exercisings of heart, ere the knee of man bends at the foot of Christ. And they are all for this very purpose, that we may be brought there, and receive what is to be had there; and get that particular fulness of blessing which can be obtained from close contact with Him.

"Why is it thus with me?" cries many a weary waiting soul, many a one knowing, as it thinks, the fulness of its need. Why but to learn, by an apparent prospect of failure in having that need supplied, that it really did not know how deep it was before? Why is it thus? Because thou must know yet more the depth of what thou dost want, and the depth of what Christ can give.

At times we think we are close enough to Christ, within reach of Him to get what we want; but He means to bring us closer still, because He intends to give us more.

The preliminaries of blessing are sometimes very wonderful; the way in which great blessings are prepared for, and come about, are amongst the deep things of God.

Although it is crowded into a short space as to time, and a few words as to the chronicling of it, yet was there much here required, ere this woman was brought into what was to be to her the place and posture of great blessing. There was the frequent repetition of those cries of anguish, when we should have said that one would have been enough—the indifference to them, and that no ordinary indifference, seeing that she cried to One who could help her (for He who can heal has, from that very power, a certain relationship to the one who requires that healing); and the natural uprising of hard thoughts about One who seemed so hard in thought to her—all this she had to undergo, but all to bring her nearer to the Lord.

Often we are inclined to say, "Why have I to bear this?" what has this to say to the blessing I need? is not this rather leading away from that blessing? But each trial is a link in the chain of blessing, inexplicable in itself, beautifully harmonious as part of a whole.

All is thus done to bring us to the feet. We must be *placed* for certain blessings. We think we can place ourselves; the Syrophœnician woman, no doubt, thought that to cry after Jesus was enough. And so it might have been, did God design no more for her than the bare healing of her child; but she needed to be particularly placed for what she was particularly to receive. The "ten lepers, which stood afar off, lifted up their voices, and said, Jesus, Master, have mercy on us. And when he saw them, he said, Go show yourselves to the priests." They received their measure of blessing thus; but she hers—and that a greater one—at the very feet.

Once at Jesus' feet there was much to follow. And it is important simply to note this, because we are apt to have very mistaken views as to finality. We are continually thinking that the end has come before it really has. We make a part of a Divine process the end, and seem surprised when it does not answer our expectation. We are seeking the blessing before it is due; we have only gone once or twice, whereas, perhaps, seven times are appointed before we see even a cloud no bigger than a man's hand.

And this is how many of God's people have been discouraged when seeking blessing. They expected too much from early stages; they never surmised that they had been brought to a certain point just in order to be led on farther.

And others are ignorant in this matter, as well as we. Their kind wishes for us are often mistaken. It is not in earthly relationships alone that we find mistaken kindness, it abounds in spiritual relationships also, so far as they exist between man and man.

It is well that we have one who has deeper thoughts for us than our friends have—thoughts which reach farther, which are fuller of blessing, which in the long run will come out with larger profit—but it must be in the long run; it is of their very nature that they must mature.

The disciples appear in this case to have been actuated by simply selfish motives. They did not want to be cried after, and therefore wished the woman to be given what she wanted, and sent away. Their idea was that in getting that, she would have got all; they did not know of anything beyond what just met the hearing of the ear—the need of the woman's child; as to any close contact with their Lord, and peculiar blessing in store for the woman therefrom—of that they knew nothing; as indeed, how could they.

Christ had deeper views for this woman than she had for herself, and so He has for us. It would have been easy for Him to have spoken a healing word, and so have ended up this matter with but little trouble to Himself, and with much satisfaction both to the disciples and the woman; but He had deeper thoughts of blessing for her than that. And so, when we do not receive all at once the good thing we desire, but are left to cry still more vehemently for it; and it may be even to be much exercised in apparent repulses with reference to it, ever let us remember that this is because God designs for us more than in this matter we have planned for ourselves. We are now in the midst of the thoughts of God as well as of our own—of His ways as well as ours; and we have to experience that His ways are not as our ways, neither are His thoughts like our thoughts.

We now have this Syrophœnician woman brought to the feet of Jesus—brought there by the apparent neglect of the One from whom she had hoped everything. Having been answered never a word, she does not, after the fashion of ordinary mendicants, go away, believing that it is but lost time to ask any more; on the other hand, she comes yet closer to Christ—closer to the One who had to all appearance practically refused her; and falling at His feet, she now bars the way, and He can proceed no further until He hear, and she knows that He hears her request; and until He answer her after some fashion. Here, then, we have her; and seeing what sort of place is the ground immediately at the feet of Jesus, how tremendous was the need of this woman, what a quoin of vantage she occupied, we may expect to hear of some very earnest work—hard conflict, if need be—ere she will give up her point and go away unblest.

The expectation is fully realised. Here we have the woman (1) remaining, (2) arguing, (3) enduring (4) persevering, and (5) conquering—and all at the feet of Jesus.

There she remained. And it will be well for us to note this; for this "remaining" has more teaching for us than we think. It is not always so easy a thing to remain quiet at the feet of Jesus; to carry on much and varied effort there; to be calm and still within the one sphere. We find it very hard to harmonise energy and calmness—to make them work together. We are for shifting the scene of operations; we are, so to speak, up and down continually; we don't continue in one stay. We should be much more calm if we realised where we were. Our power lies not so much in *what* we are, as in *where* we are. Let the feet of Jesus be to us a place of continuance.

We trouble ourselves about the amount of effort

Place for Personal Necessity. 41

we are making, whether we are earnest enough, and so forth; but in the truest need—the hardest work of the soul—there is no thought of self at all; all the eye, and ear, and thought are upon the Lord.

We never can be quiet, or put forth the power of quiet energy, unless we have well fixed before our minds the One from whom we are expecting help. Some rush hither and thither, like Balak, but they get no nearer blessing. We are to know where we are, and what is to be, and what can be done there. We have the advantage of having our field of action circumscribed, and marked out for us; now let us see what victories can be won there.

It may be that the intellectual think this position at the feet of Christ beneath them—this sphere too small for their energies. They say, "Talk to us about the head of Jesus, and not about his feet." But she who thus supplicated at Jesus' feet was thought worthy of being argued with—nay, was herself allowed to argue with the Lord, and to win in argument a victory, the like of which no lawyer has ever won in the courts, no orator in the tribune, no disputant in the schools. It was from the feet of Jesus that there was carried away the highest triumph of argument that was ever won. No excited crowds applauded; none crowned the victor; no one save her adversary in the strife gave testimony to her skill; and when it is said that *He* did, then all is said which can be said;

yea, far more than could be in all other ways beside.

Down at His feet this woman won her victory of faith—her daughter's cure. Like Jacob of old, she would not let Him go until He blessed her; like him she had power with the One with whom she strove and prevailed. Sustaining two opposite characters in the selfsame suit—plaintiff as regards her child, defendant as regards her race—she won her cause in each; a double judgment was entered in her favour by the Lord's command. If a miracle of healing proceeded from His lips, surely He must have inspired a miracle of pleading at His feet!

What had been this woman's introduction to the presence-chamber, where indeed things had fallen out so unexpectedly that, instead of simply receiving a largess as from a king, she had to argue her cause as though she had to substantiate claims in court? Poor claims they were, no doubt—the claim of the dog to eat the crumbs which fell from the children's table. But the small possessions of the poor are infinitely precious to them; their heritage of crumbs is their very life.

Her only introduction to the feet of Jesus—which, after all, was a royal presence-chamber—was by her misery. Misery is a strange chamberlain, but it is a high officer in the court of Jesus; it is one of the *grand* chamberlains, and it has authority at all times to introduce to audience with the King. Am I miserable—I ask not from what cause, but miserable—then by that very fact I am sure, if I desire it, of an immediate introduction to the presence of my Lord. The misery itself supplies the means.

Divers persons were treated differently when they came to Christ—though each one doubtless exactly as his case required; and so we cannot say, when once there, what may go on; only we know that, whatever it is, it will be exactly what is right, and what in the end will be best for us.

No doubt there are many arguings and soul-strivings carried on at the feet of Jesus. It may even be that the spirit's fiercest throes have been experienced there. And here this woman has to argue—and mark, where—at the feet of Jesus. It was when Christ might have been supposed to want to go on, she was exactly in the place where she was likely to impede Him most.

It is as though we were to be taught that Jesus has no occupations of too great moment to be arrested by human, even by individual misery. We have such occupations in action, often such pre-occupations of mind that we must not be stopped by any one, or for anything. That is just one of the differences between Christ and us.

One would have thought that while Jesus was on His feet, and kept standing there, all this argument might have been dispensed with; but He Himself, who alone could dispense with it, did not do so;

that dealing with that woman's spirit was no lost time to Him.

In all probability, in human judgment—in that of the disciples—the whole thing was most inappropriate. The woman had gone from bad to worse; whereas she had been crying after them, now she was prostrate before them.

But Christ had work to do with this woman's soul, which they knew not of; and surely He commences also in a way which they could not understand. It was a strange way to prepare for conferring a gift, by giving what seemed an unanswerable reason why the gift should not be conferred. But some of the highest gifts which men have ever had, they have come by in this way. They were emptied, that they might be filled; they were pressed hard against the earth, that they might spring up the higher from it.

Christ tells this woman that she has no national claims upon Him at all. The statement of her being a Greek, a Syrôphœnician by nation, or in other words, "a stranger," comes very quick upon the mention of "Jesus's feet," and her position at them, suggesting to us how entirely—humanly speaking—she had no business there.

But she drew an argument from her very unworthiness and alienship. She seized instantly upon that idea of the dogs, and of the children being *filled*, and of their being filled *first;* there was hope for her in these three points. She, on her part, recognised the priority of the children's claim, and their claims to fulness; but then came the claim of the dogs. Even the word used for "dogs" gave her an argument—for it was a soft, mild term the Lord used—the little dogs.

Now here we are met with a multitude of practical thoughts.

When we come to the feet of Christ, let us remember, first of all, to take up our assigned position, however low it may be. What, indeed, must be our frame of mind, how little can we know ourselves, if we are laying claim to anything in the way of position at all! We can gain no advantage by refusing to take up our assigned place—our low starting-point; we only lose time, we only lay ourselves open to the still sharper dealings of God. It may be that, we think we are put in a hopeless position by being thrust down so low; but let us remember from what depths up to what heights men have sprung—how that publican who smote upon his breast returned to his house.

This woman was put at the very extreme end of creation—the Scripture always speaking as badly as possible of "dogs," and not recognising any of their nobler qualities. It was thence—and what a "thence"—that in one bound she sprang to the forefront amongst the children of faith. Having taken something even more humble than the lowest room, she heard a voice which said unto her, "Friend, come up higher." The master of the feast set her—a stranger—above many of those who were his kinsmen according to the flesh; He gave her, not crumbs, but bread; the last became the first; and her victory of faith carried away as its lawful spoil her daughter's cure.

Let us be encouraged then to seek for much, even when under deep consciousness of our unworthiness and guilt. Let us not say, "I will seek for such and such choice blessings, when I feel myself strong as a child of God. I will put off asking any great thing until I feel myself thus strong, and am in the special enjoyment of the sense of acceptance." Let us seek for what we want as we are. Perhaps we have been placed in a depressed condition, or allowed to come into it for a while, in order that we may the more deeply feel our need, and the more earnestly, and so effectually, plead with God. Many a Christian's experience is this: "If I had not dropped so low, I had not climbed so high." Men are fond of epigrammatic mottoes for heraldry, and indeed such mottoes generally are epitomes either of history or character; if mottoes be needed for the warriors of faith, for the peerages of the skies, then can we well understand how to this woman would be assigned some such one as this.

But when we come to the feet of Jesus we are, like this Syrophœnician woman, not to allow ourselves to be overwhelmed by our need, however great; but we are to be intelligent, and to try and see things as they really are, and to recognise and make use of such hopes and openings as exist.

This woman, as we have already incidentally noticed, found three points of hope—three grounds of argument—in her own and her daughter's behalf out of the one sentence addressed to her by Christ.

Jesus said, "Let the children *first* be *filled*." The point was, not there being nothing for any one else, but that abundance must be secured for the children, and this "first." And this "first" implied a sequence. As soon as that was done an opening was made for something further; that word "first," if only the woman had power to see it, was the possible opening of a floodgate of blessing. Could we have entered the recesses of the heart of Christ, we should have heard there the echoes of the words of Hosea: "Though I lead her into the desert, yet I will speak soothingly to her. And I will grant her her vineyards from thence, and the Valley of Achor for a door of hope."

And here was this woman's Valley of Achor,*

* "Most of the Rabbins, however, and, after them, many Christian interpreters, consider allusion to be made to the name, which signifies trouble or molestation, and to this I incline. This valley had proved very inauspicious to the Hebrews on their former entrance into Canaan. They had been forced to turn their backs before the native inhabitants, and their hearts melted, and became as water: Josh. vii, 5, 8, 12, 24, 26. But on their return from the captivity, the exiles would pass through it with the undisturbed expectation of a peaceable and joyful occupation of the country. By a door of hope, is meant a hopeful entrance into the holy land."—*Henderson on Minor Prophets.*

only in her case the darkness and the light did not keep apart, but, as it were, intermingled, so that to one who could discern them, there were clouds and sunshine at the self-same time.

Now, it is a great thing to have an eye for encouragement—to see hope and openings where they are, to be quick to catch up crumbs of comfort. It is very honouring to Christ to deal with Him with a hopeful spirit—to approach Him with such; and even if things do not seem to go as well with us as we desire, still to keep it up.

We do not say that the materials for hopefulness always lie on the surface; they certainly did not do so in this case. They may have to be searched for; but, even though often it may be in the most unlikely places, they will be found. Many of God's choicest things are found in such places. There was Elijah's provision by that poor widow, and that piece of silver in the fish's mouth, and that feeding of the multitude by those five loaves and two small fishes; and here the blessing, in what at first sight one might almost be warranted in calling a curse.

In all our times of trial and depression let us be on the look out for the sun-gleams. No matter how few they are, still wonders may be done with them if they are used. The prize flower at a recent exhibition of the window gardening of the London poor was one grown in an attic, on which the sun shone for but a short time every day. But the old man who reared this plant held it up during that time to catch the beams, and turned it round and round, and won the prize. Watch for sunbeams; use them, and you shall win with them.

Believe that there is something to come; or, at any rate, that something may come. Have great faith in possibilities, especially when Christ is on the scene of action. This woman believed in the possibility of something after the "first." She did not dispute the "first," she only fixed her hope on what might come after that.

Let us avoid the mistake of undervaluing, let us see things as large as they really are.

The crumbs here alluded to, are said to be something more than what fell accidentally from the table, for it was the custom during eating to use, instead of a napkin, the soft white part of the bread, which, having thus used, they threw to the dogs.

We do not want to diminish aught from the severity of the trial of the woman's faith, or make Christ's dealing with her less sharp and apparently severe than it really was. What we say is that, here were the elements of some comfort, and it was her wisdom and blessing that she realised them.

The same remark applies to the Greek word which, when translated literally, means "little dogs." One sees in this an aggravation of the woman's trial, as though our Lord did not even think the woman and her child worthy of the name of dogs, but called them "whelps;" whereas another, and I conceive more justly, discerns in it a touch of kindness, for when, save dealing with sin, was Jesus unmitigatedly severe? That little cloud was the beginning of abundance of rain. The nucleus of blessing is often very small; crumbs picked up at the feet of Jesus turn miraculously to loaves. Never be afraid of using to the uttermost any bright thought which is suggested to you there. When Christ gives you a bright thought, or puts within your reach the material of hope, be it never so slight, it is that you may weave therewith a net to infold Him hand and foot, so that He cannot part from you without a blessing.

Thus this woman remained and argued at the feet of Jesus. Now we must add a few words upon her endurance of apparent repulse.

There was one terrible element in her trial which we must note. She was not spurned *to* the feet, but *at* the feet of Jesus. Her worst trial came upon her there. And had that woman come away unblest from that place, and had not all this been but a deep, dark defile on the highway of blessing, then we are bold to say that no man can calculate what would have been the terrible results. For proud sinners fixing on that scorn of the Lord would never subject themselves to an endurance of the like; and men of feeble hope would feel the

Place for Personal Necessity. 51

hopelessness of going there; and those of tender constitution of spirit, and of a nervous temperament, would never adventure a conflict with such roughness. But now we understand it all, or at least enough of it to make us feel there is no real cause for fear. We are on the safe and right road, though some of the stones on it are sharp.

This experience of the Syrophœnician woman tells us to avoid the mistake of always expecting dealings of unmingled brightness at the feet of Jesus. There are many strange dealings on men at times to bring them *to* the feet; are there never any strange ones when *at* them? The reader of these lines, if he know much of the spiritual life, would lay down these pages as unreal, or would receive what they have yet to say with distrust, if we made out that unmingled brightness was the characteristic of all dealings at Jesus' feet.

But, however dark may be the things which are there shown us about ourselves, blessing is not on that account about to be withheld.

When "the man, the lord of the land, spake roughly" to the patriarchs (Gen. xlii, 30) he was still their brother, and was planning great things for them. There are certain blessings, doubtless, which can come only by rough experiences. The heroes of faith, like all other truly great, have ever borne, as well as done, much. The sustainings are as wonderful as the accomplishments in the spiritual life.

When Jesus said a hard saying, "many asked who could hear it;" and when it became still more incomprehensible, "they went back and walked no more with him." "Then said Jesus unto the twelve, Will ye also go away? Then Simon Peter answered him, Lord, to whom shall we go? Thou hast the words of eternal life; and we believe and are sure that thou art that Christ, the Son of the living God:" John vi, 67, 68, 69. The faith of the Canaanitish woman, and that of the prince of the apostles, was one—they each bore up under the hard sayings of the Lord, and refused to go away.

So she persevered, and won the blessing she desired. It was on this occasion as on others—great miracles, and good doings, and outflowings of blessing followed on times of, as it were, personal withdrawings on the part of Jesus. It was after a withdrawal of Himself that the multitudes were fed, and that He appeared walking upon the waters; it was when He made as though He would go farther that He yielded to constraint, and revealed Himself as He had not done all the time He had spoken with them by the way.

All withdrawals of Christ, rightly interpreted, are real onleadings. When the bride (Cant. iii) sought her beloved, but could not find him, then she rose and went about the city in the streets; and in the broad ways she sought him whom her soul loved.

Place for Personal Necessity. 53

"It is expedient for you," said the Lord Himself, "that I go away"—for thus the Spirit came, and the heart is led onward to an ascended Christ in higher conceptions of Him than it could have had, if He had tarried here.

We would observe in closing our contemplations on this scene, how we are taught that there is mercy at the feet of Jesus for those whom we perhaps think to be outside all possible circle of blessing. The highway and the hedge teach us this: and so does this story of the Syrophœnician woman at the feet of Jesus.

Let us also see how that very often our judgment about strugglers may be altogether wrong. We know not why they are struggling, or what purposes of mercy are wrapped up in it, or how it will end. The exercises of a soul are amongst the hidden things of God. Of one thing only let us assure ourselves on these occasions, and let that reassure us: is all this really going on in the right place? for all striving must prosper in the end which is carried on at the "feet of Jesus."

CHAPTER V.

THE FEET OF JESUS THE PLACE FOR PERSONAL NECESSITY.

(MARY AT THE FEET.)

"Then when Mary was come where Jesus was, and saw Him, she fell down at His feet, saying unto Him, Lord, if Thou hadst been here, my brother had not died ;"—JOHN XI, 32.

WHEN the wind agitates the surface of a lake, in whose placid waters are reflected the mountain sides in their strength, and the sky in its beauty, their images first become broken and confused, and finally disappear.

The real mountains are there, strong as ever; and when the waters become smooth again, they will appear as they did before; but for a moment they are gone.

This is an apt image, in some respects, of what happens in our own spiritual lives. Circumstances arise which agitate us for a season, and all our tranquillity seems gone; we are no longer ourselves, we do not act in harmony with the habit of our past lives. We are wanting to our higher selves, and have to endure all the troubles which belong to an agitated state.

But in a true character there are all the elements of restoration; the strong mountains are really there; they will reassert their existence as soon as the storm is past.

Here we come upon a scene of agitation and distress; and as is so often the case, precisely where we should not have expected to find it. We should have thought that Mary would have presented us with nothing but a picture of calm. Having seen her sitting at the feet of Jesus, when Martha was so disturbed, we should have prepared to take our lesson from her in such a scene as this, in the direction of calmness, and self-possession, and peace; but it is just here, as it is in so many instances in the teachings of God, we are led by ways which we know not, the teaching comes to us in a very different way from what we expected.

We have been taught by Mary's sitting—now let us learn from her falling at Jesus' feet.

Every verse of this narrative is full of teaching—its own distinctive teaching; but we shall confine ourselves to such thoughts as suggest themselves in immediate connection with the position in which we find Mary here.

We shall first note what immediately preceded Mary's going forth to meet Jesus; and then her words and her position at His feet.

When Martha called Mary secretly she arose

quickly, and without confiding to any of the attendant mourners the reason for her acting so suddenly, as well as with such haste, she left the house. Those who mourned with her must have been astonished, but they were not long in finding out a probable cause for her conduct. She was, doubtless, seized with a paroxysm of grief, which could be relieved only at the tomb, by the nearest possible approach to the dead.

Here, as in the case of Jairus' daughter, we have a strong contrast between the many and the one—the impotence of the many—the omnipotence of the one. All that the minstrels and people could do in the one case was to make a noise; all that they could do in the other was to go after the heart-wounded one to a grave; but in each case Jesus brought with Him life, for that which we can only mourn, He can restore.

Many Jews we are told came to comfort Mary.

No doubt they were sincere in their desire to mitigate her sorrow—each had his own argument, his own aspect of comfort to present, or at least his own reason why sorrow should be assuaged; perhaps there were even some, who knew the mystery of silence, and were able to sit still, and speak not a word, save such words as looks, and the mere consciousness of the presence of sympathy can utter; but they had evidently been able to do but little, for when Mary rose hastily to go forth and meet Jesus, they thought her grief had mastered her, and that she was going to vent it at the tomb.

There is something no doubt pleasing in the thought, that rays of human sympathy should converge from a wide circumference upon one focus of sorrow. It minds us of our common humanity —that in the depths (whatever surface distinctions there may be) human kind are one—that as the poet says, "One touch of nature makes us all akin;" and no doubt all sharing of each others joys and sorrows, will prove helpful so far to our rejoining some of the myriad threads of our humanity which are broken or cut in all directions; still, sad thoughts connect themselves with the one in sorrow and the many comforters. For what the heart craves in the depth of its sorrow is not to spread itself out to many, but rather to gather itself in, and hold companionship with but few. Deep streams run in narrow water courses.

There is indeed a brawling noisy sorrow which from its very shallowness is heard here and there and everywhere, but it is different from what Mary had here.

Her heart, doubtless, sat loose to all the comforters around; and so was all the more ready to leap forth to Him who had her truest deepest sympathy, who, because He had in His keeping all the secret springs of her being could comfort her indeed.

Now, whilst we would be far from undervaluing

or casting off human sympathy, we cannot but feel conscious that it is well to sit loose to it. Or, let us put the matter in another form; we cannot but feel how little in the hour of our sorest need it can do for us. It is precious in its place; but we shall remain unsatisfied if we have no more.

Mary knew of One who was superior to *all* combined; and when He came near, she was ready immediately to leave all around, and go forth to Him. No doubt, the previous knowledge of the feet of Jesus was silently exerting its power. Those feet at which she had sat, had now approached her house; they were standing waiting for her, not very far off; she was going forth on no experimental journey—they said she was going to the grave to weep there, but she was going not to the home of death, but to the Lord of life.

It is true they were right in one respect, she was going 'to weep;' but it was one thing to weep simply at a grave, it was another to do so before the Lord of life. We may weep before each, but which it is, makes a vast difference indeed.

But we are anticipating. What we desire for the reader is, not only that he should be visited by Jesus, in the time of his sorrow, but that when Christ comes to him it should be as one well known.

Many have made their first acquaintance with Jesus in this sad time; they are happy in having done so; but they are not the happiest of all.

They are happier still, who have met him in sorrow as a well-known friend.

And for this very reason amongst others, let us now like Mary sit at the feet of Jesus, so that He may come to us as a known friend in our sorrowing times, so that we may not have to say 'Who is this that is come—who is this that is calling us out of ourselves?' but, 'it is Jesus, I will go forth at once to Him.'

And of how much—what a wonderful much can we dispense, if we have Christ Himself. Mary could leave all her friends for Him. As Jesus had meat to eat that His disciples knew not of, so Mary had a friend at hand, whose friendship was such as they knew not of.

If then in our times of sorrow and trial we would not be perhaps helplessly dependent on mere human sympathy, let us strive so to sit at Jesus' feet, that His coming to us at these sad times may draw us to Him at once. However Jesus may choose to act for us, we must leave altogether with Him—only we may be sure that, if we know Him, and are ready when He calls for us to go forth to Him; it will be always a leaving of a company of mourners to go into the presence of the Lord of life.

"She goeth unto the grave to weep there."

The many Jews had come to comfort. They recognized the deep need, which now however it seems, they are not able to supply. Mary's grief has overflowed their resources, she apparently goes to the tomb to weep there.

These friends of Mary spoke according to the probabilities of the case, doubtless according to what under similar circumstances they would have done themselves. They did not know that Mary had been called for by Jesus; nor if they had known it, could they have told how much was involved in it.

Those who do not know our connection with Jesus, do not know our resources. Their thoughts end with the natural; they can go all the length to which that reaches, but not further.

To those comforting Jews there was no point beyond that grave of Lazarus—there was no alleviation beyond weeping there. The dead was beyond all reach, but the sorrow which mourned for him, might find a home at his grave. But whatever they said, Mary does not appear to have heeded it, one thought filled her mind, and quickened her steps, that was to get into the presence of the Lord.

And now Mary has hasted and come into the presence of Jesus, and what she does is to fall at His feet—to weep; and to cry that, had He been at Bethany her brother had not died.

What Mary said and did at those feet is full of teaching to us.

And first let us look at who it is that thus hastes and cast herself down, at the feet of Jesus.

It is Mary—the calm—the contemplative—the self-possessed; the still one, who sat at the feet, who is now in such haste.

Those whom we think stillest are in truth often capable of emotion, activity, and excitement, which we should have thought utterly foreign to their nature. We often judge people as to what they possibly can do or leave undone, by the aspect in which they habitually present themselves to us, but we do not know how violently and in what an opposite direction they may be moved by circumstances.

In Mary's case there seems to have been a mingling of the natural and the spiritual—of intense human feeling, and also true spiritual sensibility; she went forth to meet Jesus, with both Lazarus and Jesus occupying chief places in her heart.

Would Jesus have had it otherwise? Would He have had her violate all the feelings of human nature? was He so jealous as not to leave any place even for the dead? did He expect her to think of Him alone when He called for her, and when He saw her hastening to His feet? No; Christ is no stifler, He is the regulator of human emotion; He had no blame for Mary; He received her as she came; He mingled His tears with hers.

Let us be careful how we form too decided an opinion about some who appear to us somewhat abstracted, and contemplative, and separated from the wear and tear of ordinary life. It by no means follows that their natural feelings and emotions are dead—that they cannot feel themselves, and feel for others. We do not know what people are, or are capable of, until the circumstances fitted to try them have occurred. When they do occur, we shall perhaps be surprised to find how full of emotion, or susceptibility to personal suffering, or how capable of sympathy such and such a person is.

Moreover let us never seek to be so contemplative, and rapt, as to be above human joy or sorrow. Whilst we are here God wills us to be men—true men, even as Jesus was. Rightly to show ourselves capable of human emotion is an infinitely truer position than to be independent or incapable of it. Neither let us seek a place at 'the feet' with the idea of raising ourselves on high from affliction. We may seek a place there selfishly, from, perhaps unknown to ourselves, a low motive as well as a high one; for our poor hearts are liable to be deceived, and what is in itself very high may be turned to a very low use; the thing may be the same, but its aim and end altogether different.

In this respect the emotion of Mary on the present occasion is very precious, and it is made doubly so by that of Jesus. Mary wept, the Jews were weeping, Jesus weeps also.

It is important to observe that He has no chiding for those tears, and that impassioned falling at

Place for Personal Necessity. 63

His feet. He has chiding for unbelief; for He presently says to Martha, "Said I not unto thee that if thou wouldest believe thou shouldest see the glory of God," (ver. 40.) It is not that He is so overcome as not to discern anything faulty which may exist; it is that within its true limits He owns the power of human sorrow as such.

And it is our belief that Jesus likes human feelings to be brought into contact with Himself.

What kind of religion is that which says, 'I will reverence Thee with the abstract, but I will keep from Thee with all that in which I most truly live, and move, and have my being?' That religion would not be the religion of our very selves, it would be unreal. Jesus would say, you are weeping about an earthly trial, a wound to your affections, a loss, a difficulty, a want; and you are not coming to Me; I am not in the reality of your daily life, but only in the creeds and abstractions of your spiritual.

It must be either because we have mistaken notions about Christ, or are not sure of Him, that we keep so aloof from Him—that we do not rise up hastily and run to Him, and fall at His feet in the passion of our souls, in the deep emotions of our life. If we knew Him as well as Mary did, we should do as she did also.

But before we part with Mary's haste, let us note two things, (1) how she sped forth to the One to whom she could unbosom herself, as soon as she knew He was at hand; and (2) how quickly she left the many comforters for the *One;* that One being in Himself of more value than all the rest.

This speedy going forth was no experiment on Mary's part. From what she had heard from Christ, sitting at His feet, she knew that her sorrow would have a place in His heart; a secret sympathy existed between her soul and His, which did not between her and all the mourners around.

Now there is no one to whom we can fully unbosom ourselves but Jesus. All deep sorrow ramifies into strata below the surface soil of human sympathy. It gets into our spiritual being; it has other life connection with us, which none but He who is God can understand; and that we feel and know.

And in truth, though men do not always know it, that is why all mere human sympathy comes short. An unspiritual man may never know this, and so never seek for anything beyond the imperfect help of his fellow man; but even a spiritually minded man may not know it either. He knows it not theologically, but he does instinctively—an instinct of his being makes him seek Christ; and in that One he finds what all 'the many' could not supply.

Thus may it be with us in our deepest sorrowing times; may we feel that Jesus is able to penetrate into those depths of our being to which the sorrow reaches, and let us bring it to Him as it is. Let us not wait until it be toned down and moderated, and, as we should think, brought into a more seemly state for His presence; but let us come to Him with our sorrows, as we must with our sins, bringing them just as they are.

Now let us inquire what Mary said when she fell at Jesus' feet.

We have no record of any formal approach, of any actual words of reverential acknowledgment; the one act of falling at her Lord's feet combined within itself at once her reverence and grief.

And in truth what she said did the same. For in those words, "Lord if thou hadst been here, my brother had not died," she declared her belief in the power and love of that Lord, and her own bitter sorrow, that because He had not been on the spot all was now hopelessly over, the beloved one had gone.

This, the saying of Mary at Jesus' feet must now occupy our attention for a little while.

We observe that the two sisters, of wholly opposite characters, both say the same thing, "Lord if thou hadst been here, my brother had not died."

No doubt this had been the burden both of the thought, and conversation of the sisters ever since their brother expired.

There had been anxious waiting ever since that touching message was sent off by the sisters to Jesus, saying, "Lord, behold he whom thou lovest is sick." Many a time, perhaps, they went out alone or together to look in the direction from which the welcome footsteps were to be expected; and questioned within their hearts, or one with the other, 'Will He come soon, why tarry His feet when the one He loves is sick even unto death?' It may be that, they watched the ebbing tide of their brother's life, and asked each other how long he could hold out, and if he could do so until the Lord should come. But the Lord came not. Weary hours stole on, but there was no sign of the One who could heal, and at last, the healing time had past, the death time came, yes, burial too; and not until all was over in the fullest sense did Jesus come.

It is no wonder then, that each of the sisters used the self-same words when the Lord appeared; for their minds, and doubtless their home words had been running in the self-same groove.

But these words are full of teaching for ourselves. And first let us note how each said, "My brother." There is something very touching in the death of Lazarus being not only a family loss, but an individual one.

The family was made up of two '*mys*.' Martha speaks of Lazarus as if he had been wholly hers, and Mary does the same; with each of them it is, "My brother." As the love had been in life, so is it spoken of in death.

Here we are brought into somewhat of a strait,

for the two remarks which we wish to make seem as though they contradict one the other.

Happy is that family where each has such property in the other, that the very habit of thought leads to the use of the word *my*.

Unhappy is that family where there is nothing but a series of "mys," where the meaning of "our" is not known as well as that of "my."

We doubt not that the 'our' as well as the 'my' was known and recognized, and that the power of it was lived in, in the family at Bethany; but now earthly grief was having its own way, and as is its custom, it concentrated the mind on personal feeling, and to some extent excluded the thought of others. And, in truth, that is one of the perils of grief—that nursing of it in our own bosom—that hugging of it to ourselves alone—that unwillingness to part with any of it, and to see that others are shipwrecked in it as well as ourselves.

Now let us contrast this 'my' of Mary, and also of Martha, with the '*our*' of Jesus.

Jesus knew that Lazarus was dead. He also knew what individual love was, for we are told that He loved Martha, and her sister, and Lazarus; they are spoken of not as the family at Bethany, but one by one; but when He speaks to His disciples about the death sleep, He says not, "*My* friend Lazarus sleepeth," but "*Our* friend Lazarus sleepeth."

Happiest is that family where many mys combine into many ours; the two—each occupying its own place, giving the ideal of the 'family' in sorrow.

"If thou hadst been here, my brother had not died." There is something very touching in that confidence, as there is in all the great confidences of love. Jesus must have felt it so. He saw His power over disease acknowledged; His love so reposed in, that it was thought impossible that it could allow any harm to happen to those who were loved; no note whatever is taken of what the virulence of the disease had been, had He only been there all would have been well.

And Jesus, we may be sure received that confidence as it was meant—the weight of the family's sorrow was not laid on Him in vain, especially when He knew that He might have been there—that He had purposely delayed.

One would have thought that Jesus would have been cut to the heart at hearing such words as these, when He knew well that He might have averted all this sorrow; and that it was owing to purposed delay on His part that Lazarus had died. But He was quite calm. We see that He was, by what happened between Him and Martha, when she used these self same words; and when He replied to them.

We see here plainly how some of love's true thoughts may however be only surface ones. Love is not the less real because it is shallow in the

Place for Personal Necessity. 69

reach of its thought; it may be untrue in its reasoning, and ill-informed as regards its knowledge, and yet be sterling and real in itself.

Now confidence—the confidence of love, even with a mistake, may often be better than suspicion with accuracy and correctness.

Our mistakes concerning Christ are our ignorance; and there may be much ignorance without guilt; but our want of confidence, no matter what form it assumes, is our sin. There are simple people making great mistakes, who occupy a higher place in the kingdom of God than wiser ones, who are cold and calculating, and seeking to be in their religion, we might almost say mathematically correct.

God is tender and patient with honest mistakes. If He were not, where should we be in our daily service, or our daily life.

"If thou hadst been here, my brother had not died."

And He might have been, but she did not know that; she did not know what had kept Him—we can scarcely speculate, as to how exactly she would have addressed Him, if she had.

There are many things which it is well for us not to know, concerning which, if we did know all, a strange storm might arise in our minds.

The fact is we are surrounded with "ifs" in life, they are a continual element of vexation and perplexity; it would be an amazing source of peace and comfort if we could get rid of them altogether. This word "if" has had power to distract, to set up all sorts of speculation, to open many a door to unbelief, to aggravate the circumstances of many a trial.

We sometimes conjure up all sorts of possible, and at times, impossible "ifs;" and the one as vexing as the other. We have to do with things not as they might have been, but as they have been, or as they are; most of our "ifs" are little better than suggestions of better arranged providences, as though we could have fitted matters in much better than has been the case.

In truth, many of our vexing and disquieting, and all our despairing "ifs" have a depth far below what we imagine; they go down into discontent with providence. It is not suggested that this was the case with Mary here, but it surely is so with us.

And as in Mary's case, the "if" fixed her mind entirely on the past; so in our case it does the like, hiding out the restorations and life which may be even at the very threshold.

Martha seems to have passed altogether beyond her sister in this matter; for she immediately qualifies her "if," by a "but;" "But I know that even now whatsoever thou wilt ask of God, He will give thee."

The "if" can never be safely used, except with the quickly following "but."

Place for Personal Necessity. 71

And now mark how Mary came to be at Jesus' feet. "Then when Mary came where Jesus was, and saw Him, she *fell* down at His feet." When we saw her last, she was *sitting* at those feet, now she has *fallen* at them.

Such are the vicissitudes of the spiritual life. Where we are found sitting to-day, we may be found fallen to-morrow. The place of our rest may be that of our struggle; that of our peace, may become that of our agony.

The fiercest throes of the soul have been experienced at the feet of Jesus. They have not been felt in the grosser conflicts with the tempter, but in heart sorrows with our greatest friend. It is indeed a wonderful sight to see a calm spirit—calm in the teaching learned at Jesus' feet, cast down there in bitter agony.

Whatever may be our spiritual destiny; with whatever shaking of soul we are to be tried, only let it be at the feet of Jesus. Whatever downcastings of soul, I am to experience, only let them be there—there Mary wept; and Jesus wept too

In Mary, the anguish of grief hid out for the moment the comfort she might have had. To weep in her Lord's presence, seemed all that she now could do. This was the only comfort she had, it was the natural effect of a natural feeling; and just shows us how little nature can do for us in our deep trial times.

The sympathy of feeling in Jesus was recognized. His power of help was clouded; in a word the natural was apparent, the supernatural was veiled. The time was one of great shaking of faith, and human feeling was so in the ascendant, that faith had little place given it for working at all.

We should learn from the shortcoming of this sitter at Jesus' feet; we must seek in our trial times to recognize Christ in His entirety, His power of sympathy and help. It is by looking at Jesus in the perfect balance of His nature, in its fulness, that we find peace.

No doubt it is often very little we can do when we get to the feet of Jesus under circumstances similar to Mary's. We too are so agitated that we can only fall down and weep; we also have a clouded and shortened vision; we are encompassed with perplexities and "ifs;" yes, those "ifs" occupy our thoughts more than anything else. Well! be it so; yet to those feet let us come, with our agitations and our perplexities, if we have nothing else to bring, but at any rate with our very selves.

For after all, that is the great point, the bringing of our very selves. Let us not wait to get more faith, or the power of doing better before Jesus, it is ourselves He wants.

It is quite true, better things might have been expected of us than we can show when we get there; we may not be able to act in a way at all

Place for Personal Necessity. 73

proportioned to our advantages and opportunities. We may give cause for rebuke as Philip did— "Have I been so long with thee, and hast thou not known me Philip?" but all this must be put down as so much loss and shame, and even with the loss and shame must we be found in our great agitations at the feet of Jesus.

Thither indeed must we go; and may we however unconsciously, yet so act in sorrow as to draw others with us into the presence of the Lord, and make them witnesses of His work.

We know not what wonderful things may be shown to those who are brought into the presence of the Lord. Perhaps all that we on our part can show is sorrow, and poor weak faith. Some 'ifs' and small outputtings of conscious union with Him; but we know not what He will do. Many may be brought to believe through our deep woe.

Setting aside, however, all else that has been advanced, great will be the profit of these lines, if they induce any believer in his time of agitation, when the still waters are broken up, to go just as he is, and cast himself with all his perplexity, his shortcomings of faith, and everything else at 'the feet of Jesus.'

CHAPTER VI.

THE FEET OF JESUS THE PLACE FOR PERSONAL NECESSITY.

(MARY AT JESUS' FEET.)

"And she had a sister called Mary, which also sat at Jesus' feet, and heard his word."—LUKE x, 39.

THE Word of God may be more fitly compared to a stream with all its variety of ripple, current, and depth, with all its diversity of wooded bank and pebbly strand, than to the ocean, all agitated or calm as far as eye can reach; and which, so far as we can see, either dashes itself in one long agony against the beetling cliffs, or sinks, subdued we know not how, upon the almost level shore.

The Word is full of wayfarings and restings, 'of war and peace,' of joyfulness and sighs; of darkness—from that of eventide, to that which can be felt; of lights—from that of day dawn, to the time when the sun is hot. You can hear in it the minstrelsy of the lover, and the trumpet of the warrior, the chant for the bride, the wail for the dead. The records of infancy, and manhood, and old age are there, for the Scripture contains the

Place for Personal Necessity. 75

story of man—yes, and much more is there, for it contains the story of man with God.

Even in this one subject of "The Feet of Jesus" is this great variety to be found.

Here are multitudes to be cast down in their sore need, here must come the solitary one in his woe—here is the excited agony of the mother, here the calm rest of the Gadarene; here is one neglecting to give even water, here is another supplying its place with ointment and with tears—here is man dishonouring by nailing to a cross, here is God honouring by placing an angel guard in the tomb—here is the fear of a loving apostle, and the "fear not" of a still more loving master—the feet of Jesus are unchanged, even though they be now "like unto fine brass, as if they burned in a furnace;" they were always a place of grace on earth, now are they the same in heaven.

This story of Mary at Jesus' feet is, as it were, one of the still deep pools which reflect the stars. It is not really still, for the current of the river is passing through it all the while—there was the flow of earnest life in Mary's soul, though her body was at rest. And we should have been glad to have had only to do with Mary, but that Martha comes and troubles this pool; and in part leads our minds, whether we will or no, away from the beautiful calm which her sister found at Jesus' feet. We might have wished it otherwise, yet many an one stepping in here, has found a

Bethesda, in which he has been made whole of an infirmity which he had.

Our profit must not, however, be purchased altogether at Martha's expense. From time immemorial she has afforded a theme to preachers, who would dissuade their hearers from an inordinate pursuit of worldly things; and she has suffered no little at their hands. To hear some people speak, one would think that in Martha there was no good thing, that she had not a soul above the meat she served; but he who would understand Martha's fault, as we find it here, must know something of Martha herself; and to know what she was, should be obliged to read along with this story, what is written about her in John xi.

This is the woman who said, "Lord if Thou hadst been here, my brother had not died;" who said still more, "But I know that even now whatsoever Thou wilt ask of God, God will give Thee;" who said as much as the boldest of the Apostles, "Yea, Lord, I believe that Thou art the Christ, the Son of God, which should come into the world."

We would willingly think solely of Mary and her Lord, but that is impossible; so let us range what we would to say under three heads:—

Martha,
Mary,
Christ,

in which we shall find a position taken up, attacked, defended.

But before we consider Mary at the feet—there kept by Christ, though attempted to be drawn away by Martha—let us pause a moment on the reception into their house.

Jesus "entered into a certain village, and a certain woman named Martha received Him into her house;" the 'certain' village and 'certain' woman seem vague; but there was a precision about them both in the mind of Jesus—the 'certain village' was one which contained a hospitable house for Him; and the 'certain woman' was a well-known friend.

There are houses in the world which, to the ordinary eye, are in no wise different from others, but to Christ they are the houses of His friends. Looking down now from His height of glory He knows them all. All the houses of a street are not alike to Him; in some He has a place, and in others none; in some He is known, honoured, loved, received, served, and ministered to; and in others, His name is little more than recognized, even as it might have been in hundreds of houses of Judea.

There is not a village or hamlet but that Jesus knows every house in it, in which He would be entertained.

And very humble are many of the houses of His friends—roadside cottages—often little better than what we should call hovels—but they are different to Him from all other dwellings—they are the houses of His friends.

In what light is my house viewed in heaven? is a question we may well put to ourselves. Is Jesus welcomed in it—to all belonging to it—do I wish it to be a worldly home; or a Christ-like home?

If we wish our house to be Christ's, we know His ways—what would please Him, and what would not; we may have it so ordered, as to have it one which He would recognize as a welcome place, if such a thing could happen as that at any moment He came our way.

We need not be solicitous about size, or convenience, or decoration of the earthly dwelling for the little time we shall need it; the one point to be careful about is—is my house one that Jesus knows? Aye, has He friends here? Am I, are mine His friends? are we well known to Him? is He sure of us? can I reverently say 'my house is His home?'

This is but a passing thought, but it is a useful —it may be a very blessed one.

Here then in the house of His friends, is Jesus received.

The reception of Jesus! At first sight the words would imply bustle and excitement, and the out-putting of great energies, and the making of great preparation. No doubt, it was so in Martha's

Place for Personal Necessity. 79

mind, even when Jesus came to her in the lowliness of His manhood; how much more would it be so now, when it is impossible for us to dissociate Him from His sovereignty, and all the majesty which almost from our infancy we know to be His.

This is an instance—one of the many, in which our first impressions need correcting. And this one is worth correcting, for mistaken views about how Jesus can be most acceptably received, are keeping many from courageously opening all their heart-doors to Him, and asking Him in. In truth the thought of our receiving Him, blessed and true though it be, is to be corrected and adjusted by the thought of His receiving us. Martha was full of the idea of 'receiving' Jesus; the corrective was supplied by her sister's 'being received' as a disciple and a learner, by the Lord.

To give to Jesus is a high, and indeed a natural impulse of a truly loving soul—for what kind of love is that, which does not delight in giving! but to receive from Him is something higher, deeper, better in every way. Those who can pass beyond the outward and material substance of what is received, into the invisible, subtle and delicate feeling of right receiving, with all the emotions which belong to it, know a mystery of love indeed. The ancient alchymist spent a life time in trying to turn baser substances to gold; but love's alchymy can turn a wild flower with no garniture but a dew drop, into a more precious gift than sprays set with the most glittering of gems.

This is beautiful—but it is rare; and it gives us a glimpse of how much of what is noble and precious, God has made possible to be linked to common things; and of how all this nobility and preciousness may be the property of the poorest as well as of the richest and great. But we must not follow out the thought.

To return to the scene before us here, Jesus, who ever leaves a gift where He has been, will correct the exaggerated importance of giving, when put into competition with receiving; it is a deep lesson—one, the bare idea of which many can be scarce got even to take in; but He knew its price, and He would teach it to the loved ones here.

Christ would correct the mistake as to what will please Him most. He would shew us, as we shall see presently, that we are likely to misunderstand Him. Martha's blame and Mary's praise are for all time—they are for the Church—they embody principles which in truth are everlasting.

Now, let us as we proposed, look at all three in order—and first as to Martha. Much has been said about the natural characteristics of these sisters. Martha has always been considered a woman of an active, bustling, energetic disposition; and so, no doubt, to a great extent she was.

And expositors have frequently seen nothing more than these; and so have failed to draw any teaching from the narrative, except that, 'it is bad to be too much taken up with the things of time and sense.'

We accept this as in part a description of Martha's character, and we desire to profit by the practical lesson grounded on it; but allowing full room for the difference between the natural characteristics of the sisters, we must go below them to discover the true teaching which we have here. They were sisters in blood—and, as we see in John xi, in faith; but they were dissimilar in character and temperament, and more important still, in depth of spiritual perception and attainment. This last is the true key to the story; and we have to deal, not with a worldly and a spiritual person as antagonistic the one to the other, but with two dear children of God, and lovers of Jesus, only in different stages of development; and so, looking from different stand points at their Lord.

As our concern now lies with Mary rather than Martha, we may content ourselves with this statement, only drawing attention to a teaching from the fact that Martha and Mary were sisters, and dwelling in the one house.

If between these two, dwelling under the same roof, we perceive such a difference; what diversity may we not expect to find amongst many—all in the same Church. And let us beware of falling

G

in our own day and amongst those with whom we have to do, into the mistake which is so commonly made about the sisters of Bethany. As people forget the 11th of John, and almost degrade Martha from being a disciple at all; so are some inclined to almost unchristianize those whose experience is not the same as theirs. We may, indeed, recognize the troubling about many things, we may not sympathize with it, we may have risen above it; but the Martha we despise is dear to Jesus; yea, (even as in the 11th of John,) she can on an emergency rise to a great height of faith—our readiness to disown each other in the large circle of the Church of God whether from the Martha or the Mary side, may find its correction here.

Let the reader also note the different degrees of attainment in these two sisters. And with the difference of attainment came that of development and practice. It was not in all probability that Mary loved Jesus any more than Martha, but her spiritual apprehension and the development of her spiritual life were greater. So is it often now—spiritual apprehension is not always abreast of personal affection; no doubt this causes loss, but thanks be to God it does not invalidate love.

But now we pass to

Mary. She was the one found at the feet of Jesus, and therefore with her we have principally to do.

First then, as to the position she took up. It is sometimes helpful to look at what a thing is not, as well as at what it is.

This was not an indulgence of sentimental affection towards Christ; nor of personal ease as regards herself. Either would have put her in the place of rebuke instead of defence. Christ would have estimated the first at what it was worth; and the second He would have severely condemned. In all probability, had either been the position of Mary at this time, He would have answered her sister's complaint very differently from the way in which He did, and told the one at His feet, to stir herself, and attend to her part, in that at least which was needful, in the household work.

There is a certain kind of sentimental affection towards Christ, which may be taken for solid love; but He knows exactly what it is, and does not countenance it. Mere sentimentality is a sickly washy thing, and confers no honour on the Lord.

In truth what Mary had was the highest of all activity, that of the mind and soul. She was all alive in them—to outward appearance she was sitting at Jesus' feet, but her inmost being was waiting upon Him with all its powers.

She had more to do with action than her sister knew. For what was she then doing, as she sat at the feet of Jesus, but receiving those blessed seeds of truth into an honest and good heart, which were doubtless destined to mature into after action. Martha's love was shewing itself in giving what could be seen; Mary's, in taking in the unseen—Martha's was spending itself, Mary's was gathering in for greater spending by and by.

Mary, we may be sure, knew more than Martha of the inner mind of Jesus; that it was His great pleasure to give and not to receive — that the daintiest meats of this world were nothing compared with the least nourishment of the soul—that His very presence allowed of lawful expectation. She took up the position of a receiver of loving-kindness—an embracer of opportunity—an expecter of out-flowings of love. She was, in truth, a great honourer of the wayfaring—the outcast—and almost wandering Jesus. The position which the great men of her country despised, was the very one she took up—at the feet of Jesus.

And how came she to do so? She had evidently seized an opportunity. And why did she?

Perhaps Jesus had begun to speak, and attracted by what He said, she placed herself where she should not miss a word; or it may be that, from former experiences of Him, she at once took up the loving listener's place, expecting, that as formerly, so now, she should get blessing.

It was a position in which she made much of Jesus, in the way in which He wishes to be made much of; in which she manifested the higher appreciation. Had Mary not been sitting all eager and intent at Jesus' feet, she would have been with Martha in full activity of service. She is only not with Martha for Christ, because more immediately with Christ Himself. She saw Jesus in His true character, the giver rather than the receiver—the One honoured more by receiving from, than giving to.

And how far do we know this truth? How far have we entered into what we might call the constitution of Jesus? Can we perceive that 'giving' is almost as it were a very necessity of His life.

Our little spendings have their place, and a very blessed one in the mind of Jesus; but we must never put them in competition with Him; nor may we allow them to take the place of His.

But alas! are there not some, who are neither giving to Jesus, nor receiving from Him, into whose house, whose heart, He has never come.

If, by any means this be so with the one who reads these lines, let it be so no more.

There is no one who will value what you do for Him as Jesus will; no one who will give to you as He will; no one who will consecrate your house as He will.

Do not say that you must be of the world, for your business or your family leave you little time for Christ. Nay, even in the world be for Jesus. See the price He put upon the heart; and even if you cannot do much for Him, let Him do much for you.

Let Him be welcome in your house, and if you have no house, then in your room; and if you have no room, then by your bedside, or to your thoughts, as you lie upon that bed itself.

But chief above all, let Him be welcome to your heart—there be His house, where He is received with honour and joy, finding in blameless, yes, in honoured balance, the ministerings and the listenings, the activities and the rest of love.

The position thus intelligently taken up by Mary, is now attacked by Martha. It was then as it is now, who can quietly and unquestioned take up a position of peaceful learning at 'the feet of Jesus,' without its being disturbed by somebody!

There is evil enough in this mistaken attack of Martha's, without more being added to it by expositors. She was not wholly engrossed with selfishness as some would think; probably she was not selfish in the matter at all; nor was she of necessity intent on making a display; she was for honouring her Lord, only in her own way; and that was not the way most acceptable to Him.

There was that which was good, and there was that which was bad, in her assault. There was her desire to honour Christ, but there was the ignorance of the way in which He could be more highly honoured; there was the dogmatic putting of her own standard of duty—a duty which she was endeavouring to perform even beyond her strength; but there was also a non-recognition of anything higher, of anything beyond.

It is just what we see every day; and what, if we be not on our guard against it, we find creeping continually upon ourselves. And the more we are individually interested in any branch of work, or in any experience of feeling, the more likely are we to make it the standard for all others.

Martha wished Christ to be served in her own way; she was intent on it. It may be that, in part she was under the influence of her natural character as an active housewife, and wished that all that housewifery could do should be put forth; but then it was for the honour of her Lord. Those dishes were to be dressed for and set before Him. And so far the thought was good.

Overstrained good may, however, become evil—some of the most subtle and best masked evil is nothing but this; and Martha so magnified her own position and work as to have no eye for, no understanding of, Mary's.

She had no calm judgment; and probably after some waiting, and some considerable preliminary kindling of the fire, at last she spake with her tongue; and ran, so to speak, full tilt against Christ Himself. "Carest thou not," (ομ μελλει "is it nothing to thee,) that my sister hath left me to serve alone?" Martha did what many an one attempts now—she tried to enlist Christ in her quarrel. She would have made Him a partizan.

Martha thought she was strong in the feeling and judgment which He must have on the matter, and in the claims of human relationship, "my sister," "me;" yes, and in the mixed feelings of indignation, and justice, and pity, which are summed up in the word 'alone;' and in truth, the onslaught was severe; and had there not been something more powerful to counteract it, must have prevailed.

Like Martha, we are often going further than we think; we are unconsciously but really wounding Christ Himself. We are for dragging Him into conflicts which are utterly distasteful to Him; we are arguing petty claims of our own, and bringing them into competition with His; my sister—my husband—my wife—what they have to do with me, and not what they have to do with Christ.

The defence of this position by Christ was a discriminating and a decided one.

Jesus did not ignore Martha; He noted all about her, and defined her position—as well as Mary's. The perception and statement of Mary's immeasurable superiority did not induce Him to pour contempt on Martha, whose fault was, not work, but being overburthened in it. Here, Jesus gave us the true rule of action. We must never despise, never ignore the position of an adversary, or the adversary himself. On the contrary, we must enter as far as possible into His views of matters, before we judge them.

Jesus notes that Martha would have supplied Him with many things—for whom were they all, but for Himself! but they brought on her care, and trouble; she let her natural energy no doubt go out into them, but it had overwhelmed her.

Jesus knows the caring and the troubled ones, as well as those who are in deeper fault; on the one side He will not fail to condemn an error, because it is entertained on His behalf; on the other, He will not, because it is an error, refuse to give credit for what there is in it of good.

But Jesus was very decided; it "shall not be taken away from her." I will not take her good part away from her—you shall not—circumstances must not.

No; Jesus will never send us forth from Himself, to be drawn round in a whirlpool. I do not say He will not send us forth in proper season to work, even as he did the demoniac; but He will not fall in with the mistakes of energetic people, as they would wish. Martha would have involved Mary in the same whirl that she was in herself. Therefore there is great encouragement here to our aiming at some close communion with the Lord. He will not send us away. He knows the longing of our souls; that we are craving to be fed and taught of Him; that we feel none can satisfy us but Himself; and blessed are such hungry ones, for they shall be filled.

Thus, they who gather themselves in to rest in

Christ, have no need to fear that they will be unduly disturbed by Him. At the proper time He will send them forth to their work as He did the demoniac; but He will not have them vexed for every excitement that comes the way. And as He will not Himself take away the rest of His people, no more will He allow others to do so. Martha sought a commission so to do to Mary, but Jesus refused to give it.

And there are some who seem to have a vocation for stirring up every body, and almost every thing, too. They know neither the power nor the pleasure of rest; their tremendous energy, or their irritable restlessness, would carry away, or fret others whose chief power and life is in the peace of God; from such we may take refuge in Christ Himself.

But He will do even more than give us this. He will defend us from circumstances. He says, 'they also shall not take you from peace.'

Now, it often happens that circumstances appear to involve great need; and to call upon us to engage in them. But is this need always so real? is the necessity invariably laid on us? Some persons think so; and the consequence is that they scatter themselves, and lose their self-possession, and become shallow; they are to be found in every thing; they are in things, but where are they in themselves?

The apparent need is not always a real one; it was not so here. Had it been, Christ would have sent Mary at once to her sister's help; but He refused to fall in with Martha's mistake. Christ discriminated and judged in this matter; and He will teach us to do the same.

But the Lord's defence of Mary was reasonable, as well as decided. It might be said, was not Mary to be jealous of the honour of the house as well as Martha; of its hospitality; of Christ's having the very best in every way which it could afford; that best, made the best indeed by all the care and pains which they could bestow upon it?

Yes! Mary was as jealous of the honour of the house as Martha; but she had so overpassed her in spiritual apprehension that, she knew that to be at the Saviour's feet was more acceptable to Him, than to be engaged in preparing many dishes for Him.

She had not grasped the great outlines of truth any more clearly or boldly than Martha; the 11th of John would teach us that; but the spiritual perceptive faculty was more delicate with her, and it enabled her to discriminate between seeming neglect and real honour.

Mary was in truth giving far more than Martha; she was giving her very self,* in that form which is

---

* On this giving of ourselves, Abp. Leighton has the following beautiful words :—" Let us give Him (God) ourselves, or nothing ; and to give ourselves to Him is not His advantage, but ours. As the philosopher said to his poor scholar, who, when others gave him great gifts, told him he had nothing but himself to give. ' It most precious to Christ—as a receiver of Himself.

In the last day will it come out how much some have given—some who were little known in outward activities.

And great encouragement may be gathered here for those who have not much outward to give. Some are prevented by illness, by circumstances, from doing much. We do not say their case is that which is spoken of here; but that they also may gather incidentally some comfort.

Every one who has himself, has much to give; every one who can appreciate Jesus, listen to Him, choose Him, lovingly trust Him—has, in all that, opportunity of honouring the Lord. Such may be misunderstood, or possibly despised, by the world, but they will be vindicated by Him.

Had we not intended to speak of the Lord

is well,' said he, 'and I will endeavour to give thee back to thyself better than I received thee.' Thus doth God with us, and thus doth a Christian make himself his daily sacrifice: he renews his gift of himself every day to God, and receiving it every day bettered again, still he hath the more delight in giving it as being fitter for God, the more it is sanctified by former sacrificing. Now that whereby we offer all other spiritual sacrifices, and even ourselves, is love. That is the holy fire which burns up all, sends up our prayers, and our hearts, and our whole selves a burnt-offering to God; and, as the fire of the altar, it is originally from heaven, being kindled by God's own love to us; and by this the Church, and so each believer, ascends like a 'straight pillar of smoke' (as the word is, Cant. iii, 6,) going even up to God 'perfumed with aloes, and all the spices, all the graces of the Spirit, received from Christ; but, above all, with His own merits:'" *Leighton.*

Place for Personal Necessity. 93

separately, some of what we are now about to say would have been noticed when considering Mary. Jesus Himself was mistaken and misjudged. "Is it nothing to thee?" said Martha. She formed a wrong judgment of Christ. She did not see those deeper interests, that greater honour, that profounder relationship, which He did; and which He recognized by keeping Mary at His feet.

This is exactly how it comes to pass that, we so often wrong the Lord. It is simply out of shallowness and ignorance.

We, in point of fact, often say to Him, 'dost thou not care?' 'is it nothing to thee?' because He is not acting for us, or by us, as we will, we charge Him with thoughtlessness of us.

"That my sister hath left me to serve alone!" She only saw her sister in relationship to herself—not to Christ! and put in her claims accordingly. No doubt it was in order that, Christ should be served with the many things that Martha wanted Mary's help; but she brings herself 'as left,' prominently forward; and in the mention of "my sister,"—the human relationship, we see a claim put in, in competition with Christ's.

If mere man had been in the Lord's place, knowing as much of his own real claims as He did, how differently would he have acted. He would, in all probability, have fired up in indignation; he would have asserted the claims of his personal dignity; but Jesus vindicates Mary and not Himself. He passes by the personal affront, 'dost thou not care;' and throws His shield over the one who sat listening at His feet.

Jesus was here, as ever, forgetful of His mere self. So far as principle was involved, and truth, He vindicated them by the way in which He spoke of the better part; but He did not notice Martha's attack upon Himself.

There are many teachings for us in this.

We are taught to vindicate truths rather than ourselves; to pass by what is merely personal, even though it be unjust. This is very hard to do; still Jesus did it, and that, often under circumstances of great provocation; let us try to do the same.

We see here how He put the hunger and thirst of Mary's soul and its refreshment before those of His own body, and its entertainments, His contentment with what was simple, His forgetfulness of self in the willing loss of an elaborate feast. Martha, if she could have seen it, together with Mary at His feet, and but a single dish to satisfy hunger, would have been more acceptable to Jesus than all the preparations which both Martha and Mary could have made.

And so, there is great encouragement to us to invite Jesus in our poverty. However humble may be our circumstances, if we have ourselves to give, we have what He requires; for He seeks not ours but us.

And it is important to observe His recognition of the worth of that which is communicable from Himself. He vindicates those who are appreciating Him, not feebly, or theoretically, or as a matter of course, but in the full power of the consciousness of how wise they are—what good they get.

He knows that they get good from Him as distinguished from channels; that there is a deep need of our union with His very personality; that there is a communion with Himself which is independent of all channels; and with the full presence of these before the mind, He defends those who appreciate being near His very self.

It is of as much importance to us that Christ should know how well He can supply, as that He should know how great is our need; His riches, as well as our want. For He will always put the two together; each would be strong alone; but each acquires fresh, yes, doubled strength, when brought into connection with the other.

And it will be well for us to act on this knowledge. Let us often plead Christ's wealth with Him; let us bring it forward as a reason why much should be poured out to us; let it excite our expectation. The more people have on earth, the more is expected from them; the more we know of Christ's wealth, the more should we expect from Him.

We should not stop at ever thinking about our

poverty. We may think about this until we grow morbid; until we have no capacity for thinking of anything higher; until we are so depressed, that we come to content ourselves with bearing it. But Jesus would not have us content in this; He never says, 'know thyself to be poor,' unless it be to add, 'that I may make thee rich.' When He corrects the mistake of the Laodiceans, and tells them that they are wretched and miserable, and poor, and blind, and naked; He adds, "I counsel thee to buy of me gold tried in the fire, that thou mayest be rich, and white raiment, that thou mayest be clothed." Jesus is too considerate, too tender-hearted, too noble, to remind us of our deep poverty, unless He were willing to relieve it.

We can believe that Jesus thinks with great happiness of all the fulness and riches in Himself; that "it pleased the Father that in him should all fulness dwell." And in this thought of His fulness and exceeding wealth, His people have large place. It is all for them. The true secret of pleasure in the possession of wealth, is to have it for the purpose of giving. The pleasure of hoarding is a pleasure of sin. Jesus hoards nothing; what He has, and is communicable to His people, He does communicate; and doing this is joy to Him.

A part of the defence of Mary consisted also in Christ's visibly bearing that she should in one sense leave Him unserved; in His allowing the position she took up. He was content to forego the lesser, for He knew that the greater was present.

And Jesus is the same now as He was in Mary's time; He will be to us even as He was to her. There are invisible and quiet receptions and teachings *now*, even as there were at Bethany, when Mary sat at Jesus' feet.

CHAPTER VII.

THE DEMONIAC.

(PART I.)
(HOW THE DEMONIAC CAME TO BE AT THE FEET OF JESUS.)

"Then they went out to see what was done; and came to Jesus, and found the man, out of whom the devils were departed, sitting at the feet of Jesus, clothed, and in his right mind: and they were afraid:"
LUKE viii, 35.

IT is a skilful hand which can produce a perfect picture with masses of cloud above, and with darkness in the foreground as well as in the background; the whole of the picture's light being concentrated on two figures with dazzling brilliancy.

This St. Luke has accomplished here; and he could not have done it had not the material been supplied to him direct from heaven.

Everything here is black—the demons, the swine, the conduct of the Gadarenes—but, lit up with an intense light, is to be seen Jesus, and the man out of whom the devils were departed, sitting at His feet.

This man is to be our study now—(1) how the man came to be at those feet; (2) the man as he was there; (3) as he *was seen* there; and (4) as he was sent away from there.

And in inquiring into how this man, known as "the devil-possessed," both far and near, came to be found at such a place as "the feet of Jesus," and under such altered circumstances—"sitting," "clothed," and "in his right mind"—our minds revert to the figures in the picture, with which the chapter opens.

It is by no chance, by no hasty and unskilled manipulation of the brush, that such figures could be produced. There are inherent difficulties which present a resistance to the artist. We might say, there is a preliminary resistance to be overcome, and a preliminary process to be gone through. Both these we find here. Let us, so far as we can, trace the working in of the immediate background, which by its darkness throws out the figures of Jesus and the demoniac sitting at His feet. We shall confine ourselves to this; and, it may be, as we proceed, the reader will find that some of the dark colours which are mixed are those with which he is, from sad experience, only too familiar himself.

This man did not come into his sitting posture at Jesus' feet without preliminary resistance, and that resistance presents us with three important characteristics. It was the resistance of darkness, of effort, and of debased intelligence. We have these three ingredients well defined.

The man was in a state of utter darkness as regards Jesus; not as regards who He was, for St. Mark tells us (v. 6) that, "when he saw Jesus afar off, he ran and worshipped Him, and cried with a loud voice, and said, What have I to do with thee, Jesus, thou Son of the most high God?" but as regards His character and mission; his only idea of Jesus was that of His being a tormentor.

That the man had an awfully debased intelligence we shall see presently; but, co-existent with that, was his profound darkness.

When it is put in so many plain words, we are startled at the idea of a man calling Jesus a "tormentor." From our youth up, we have always heard of His sweetness and tenderness, and of His invitations to the weary and the heavy-laden to come to Him, and He will give them rest; and there is scarce any one professing to be a Christian who would not shrink horror-stricken from the blasphemy of calling Him in plain terms so fearful a name; but underneath the thin gilding of nominal Christianity, we soon come to the debased metal of the natural heart; the only real idea of many a one is, that He is his tormentor. This is one of the hard speeches which the hearts of ungodly sinners have spoken against Him; and concerning which He will execute judgment, when He cometh with ten thousands of His saints.

It may seem hard to some that, they should be held accountable for speech which they have never

The Place of Rest.

uttered with their lips. They say, 'Human laws do not take note of any but overt acts.' But the law which has to do with your souls takes note of the libels of the heart; it hears a voice out of the depth of the darkness of our inner feelings and desires say of Jesus, as the crucifying crowd said, "Away with Him," or, as the demoniac howled out, "Torment me not."

The pressing home of the truth, the immediate and undeniable presence of Christ, the feeling that a man has to do, not with what he has read or heard of Christ, but with His very self, brings out what he really thinks of Him by nature—that He is a tormentor—torment me not.

It is the work of the prince of darkness; it is the great lie of darkness; there, in darkness about what Jesus is, does the evil one like to keep the soul; and such is the utterance he delights to hear it make. Indeed, this heavy dull resistance of darkness, and misapprehension, is the first great impediment to Christ's true work upon the soul.

No wonder that people do not want to have any close dealing with Him, when they think of torment and discomfort—that so many young people will have nothing to do with Him, saying, 'If I become what people call a Christian, I shall lose all my pleasures;' and so many older ones say, 'And I shall not be able to devote myself so thoroughly to my business, making it all in all to me as it is now.' The heart that loves says, 'If I answer this claim of a higher love, those who now have my affections cannot have them as thoroughly as they had before. Jesus, we adjure thee, torment us not. We will not do anything openly against thee, but do thou nothing against us; torment us not.'

This poor demoniac did not know that, Jesus never took but to give—never emptied but to fill. He had no idea of there being anything beside wandering in the tombs; and thought that to lose even that wretched existence, would be, perhaps, to go out into the deep. He was like many now, who think there can be no change from what they have or are, to what is better; but that the loss of these is the loss of all.

This was one point of resistance which had to be overcome, before the demoniac could be brought to the feet of Jesus.

As might naturally be expected, the passive resistance of opinion issued in the active one of effort.

What strength this man had, and indeed it was terrible, he put into his rejection of Jesus—he "cried with a loud voice."

It may seem to us that, there is nothing wonderful in this, seeing the man was a demoniac—that the loud cry is what was to be expected from him. And just because it was what was to be expected, is it likely to escape our notice in the teaching which it has for ourselves. He was under demon

The Place of Rest.

rule; and it is the law of demon nature that it should put forth all its strength against Christ.

In this case, the cry was outward and audible; but such cries are now often to be heard in the spiritual world, though, as far as mere human hearing is concerned, all is silent; or there may be even a passive endurance of the presence of Christ.

The ears of Him who can hear the heart's real voice are smitten with the cry, "Art thou come to torment me?" "what have I to do with thee?" Though men know not what they are saying, they are in truth crying out, 'Leave me as I am. I prefer to be torn and to cut myself with stones, to range the mountains in nakedness, and to dwell amongst the tombs to having anything to say to Thee.'

There is One who judges not after the seeing of the eye, nor after the hearing of the ear; and He hears voices which appear to join in family worship, and to mingle with the psalmody of His Church, crying out from the heart's real depths, "What have I to do with thee, thou Son of the living God?—art thou come to torment me?"

There is something very awful in the energies of a man's nature being gathered up in resisting Christ—in the loud voice so ready to rise against Jesus; especially when compared with the feebleness of the voices which rise for good.

And in the day of great account, when the history of the soul's transactions with Jesus shall be disclosed, how many will there be who will then for the first time discover, to their horror, the amount of energy they had put into their rejection of Jesus—how loudly they repudiated—how loudly they cried out against Him!

That loud voice of the demoniac, however startling to others, was not so to himself—he was accustomed to "crying;" and so it may be with man now; he may cry long and loud, and yet unabashed, against Jesus. Satisfied with his own state, a man may all the while be crying out against the Son of God, and pouring the blasphemies of the heart into listening ears in the other world.

The resistance offered by the demoniac to Christ was not, however, one of simple violence. The evil spirits, when they entered into the *swine*, acting in a manner suitable to the nature of the creatures in which they were lodged, impelled them violently down a steep place into the deep; but when in the *man*, they wrought through a debased intelligence. The demoniac said, "What is there to me and to thee?"—*i.e.*, what have we in common?

He recognised the existence of distinct and widely divergent paths for himself and Jesus; and embodied the thought energetically in the loudness of his cry. Of all the cries wherewith that man made the solitude of the graves ring again, there was not one, into which he more terribly put his

The Place of Rest.

whole being than this. And although it be not accompanied with loud cries, or be shouted out to the world; yes, even though on the other hand, the spiritual demoniac be a cunning rather than a violent man, and try to hide his principle of action from the world, still he who stands out in opposition to Christ, does so upon a like foundation with the demoniac here.

The foundation of all rejection of Jesus is the deep inward feeling that we have nothing in common with Him; and, moreover, that we do not wish to have.

A man sees that Christ's ways are not as his ways; and that for him and Christ to come together is like the meeting of fire and water.

There are numbers of men who would be content to have Christ, if they could keep their old selves also; but they know enough to feel they cannot; and so they bid Him go.

This man took up a demoniacal standpoint, from which he viewed himself; putting himself as a devil-possessed out of the common family of manhood, and denying that he had aught to do with Jesus the Son of the Most High God.

Now from what standpoint did Jesus view this man? He took him, we conceive, in the twofold power of His being the Son of God and Son of man.

This demoniac, when he cried, "What have I to do with thee?" put a question to which he thought there could be but the one answer—viz., "nothing," but to which Jesus knew there was another; and in that other lay the man's deliverance and life.

The one thus possessed of devils, and directly challenging Christ with this question, was a *man*, and Jesus was '*Son of man*,' as well as Son of God.

Horrible as was the condition of the devil-possessed, there was a point of common humanity and interest between him and Christ. The human nature thus degraded, was the same as that which sinlessly belonged to Jesus himself. And Jesus recognised the humanity of the man. He said, (Mark v, 8,) "Come out of the *man*." The man's identification of himself with the devils, "My name is Legion: for we are many"—that, coupling together and intermingling of the "I" and "we," is not recognised by Jesus; He severs the man from the spirits, and sets him free as a man again. "Thou unclean spirit, come out of him!"

It is well—yes, it is essential to our spiritual life, even to our salvation, to be strong on the subject of the Godhead of Jesus; it is equally necessary that we should be strong on that of His manhood. Nothing is to be gained by our impairing in the slightest degree the perfect humanity—and the completeness of the humanity—of Jesus. On the other hand, there is great loss; for if Jesus be not full man, human sinfulness apart, the key to infinite treasure is lost. Where is our Sympa-

The Place of Rest.

thiser? where our experienced Friend? where our very Sacrifice?

To detract from the fulness of Christ's manhood is as much to disturb the harmony and full proportion of His being, and to wrong and misunderstand Him, as to detract from His Godhead. Touch His perfect Godhead, or His perfect manhood, and you have no longer the Christ of the Bible; nor, we may add, the Christ of your own need.

And descending from Jesus to ourselves, we may repeat a portion of this observation. There is nothing to be got by impairing the dignity of manhood; even as, on the other hand, nothing is to be had by exaggerating it. There are opposite schools of thought by which each of these errors are taken up. He who would know what man really is, must hold part of what is held by each.

One practical point, however, is suggested to us here by Christ's recognition of the man, and His refusal to acknowledge the obliteration of humanity by the indwelling of the devils. It is this:—

As man, with all the great possibilities of manhood, with all its privileges, with all His own community with it, His own interest in it, you are before the Lord. He is predisposed to look favourably upon you. Your very humanity goes for much with Him; it is important in His eyes. Jesus does not acknowledge the right of evil beings or propensities to have possession of you. How completely then have all who would struggle against evil the sympathies of Jesus on their side! How is He willing that the nature which He Himself bears in all sinlessness should be rescued from evil in every way! How have we with us the Son of God, and Son of man!

And then, forasmuch as our eyes must be kept closely upon Jesus, mark how this man was saved by what was in that Holy One, and not by anything in himself. He was so clouded as to his state, so overridden with evil, that all which came forth from him was the cry of repudiation of any oneness with the Lord; but the clear eye of Jesus saw all; and out of the love and pity of His own heart, He acted, and called back the man to true manhood, yes, and to His own feet. It was Jesus' view of the man's necessity, and not his own, that did it all.

And thus there came an end to the terrible "often" of which we read—the binding with fetters and chains, the plucking asunder and breaking in pieces of those bonds, the futile efforts of man to tame him. All the man's sufferings, his double woe, from the tyranny of the devils, from the discipline of his fellow-men, were ended.

From all suffering there is a voice of comfort, if we be skilled to catch its tones; and they are to be found here.

We know perhaps the meaning of the word "often," sadly know it, in our own history, and in that of dear ones, whom over and over again we have attempted to control, but all in vain.

This "often" is found more or less in the history of every soul; how terribly in that of some! perhaps, how terribly in our own!

But Jesus can deal with our "oftens" as well as with our "seldoms," the latter frequently as bad as the former.

We mention them as embracing all our need, our omissions and commissions, our violence and our apathy, our all of evil, whatever it may be; therefore, let us take courage.

Man has failed. We have failed with others, with ourselves; the remembrance of the "often" is overwhelming us. We have expended all known means—fetters and chains—for binding up evil. Let us remember this demoniac's "often," the "often" of his friends, and where we found him at last—at the feet of Jesus.

CHAPTER VIII.

(PART II.)
(THE DEMONIAC SITTING AT THE FEET OF JESUS.)

EVEN the greatest events often make impressions on us wholly inadequate to their real importance. We do not care to inquire into how they came about—how wonderful they really are—what great results hang upon them. We are struck by some few of the leading features, but we are not concerned to inquire into the minutiæ.

The crowds who line the streets, and fill the balconies, and cluster on the house-tops, when a victorious army is returning to the capital in triumph, are, perhaps, intoxicated with the pageant; it passes amid a whirl of excitement and storm of applause, but how few think of all that it involves—the patient drill, the working together of so many brains, the union of so many hearts and hands and minds, the forethought, the self-denial, and the skill.

And still fewer think of all that hangs upon this success—the political changes, the effects upon national character, the misery or welfare of their fellow-men, as the case may be.

And thus exactly is it with regard to the story of the demoniac, who is here presented to us, as sitting at the feet of Jesus. There he is, a sufficiently wonderful object to attract our attention, and excite our wonder; but how few think of all which, as we have seen, happened, ere he was brought there; and of all that, for himself and others, hung upon his wondrous change!

We have seen something of what was involved in the demoniac's coming to be at the feet of Jesus at all; now let us contemplate him as he is sitting there.

The demoniac presents himself to us under three different aspects: he is (1) a changed, (2) a resting, and (3) a satisfied man.

He is, as it were, a ray of light emanating from Jesus; and just as a ray, the moment you pass it through a prism, breaks up into a diversity of beautiful colours, so the work of Christ, when examined, divides itself into component parts, each one distinct, but each harmonizing with the other.

The demoniac might easily, as sitting at Christ's feet, be presented to us in as many aspects as there are colours in the prismatic ray; even then the subject of his change would not have been treated exhaustively, but these three will suffice for the purpose immediately in hand.

The demoniac was a *changed* man indeed. His cure was perfected at once; and so he is presented to our notice, as being a complete and startling contrast to what he had been before. He nad been violent, he is now calm; he had been naked, he is now clothed; a few moments before he would have nothing to do with Christ, now he is sitting at His feet; he loved to dwell amongst the tombs, now he sits at the feet of the One whose voice the dead in their graves shall hear, and live—the spoiler of the sepulchre, the Resurrection and the Life.

We may crouch at the feet of Jesus in abject terror, or sit there in satisfying rest. The man had done the first, and now he does the last. As in many a case, there was a falling before there came a sitting. It was with him as it was afterwards with Paul.

The reader will observe that we are speaking of the contrast of a completed cure. And we are anxious to state this, because so many say that nothing is done unless all be done. We have shown how little sympathy we have with this idea, by tracing the preliminary process through which this man went, and the all importance of his debased humanity being brought into contact with the man Christ Jesus, the SON OF THE MOST HIGH GOD.

Every approach to Christ is precious, every dealing direct with Him is hopeful. We know not what *may* come out of it; there may, no doubt, be rejection of Him, as by the Gadarenes, but there may be healing from Him, as there was for the dweller amongst the tombs.

The demoniac is a changed man in his whole being—*externally* and *internally;* he is clothed as regards the body without; he is in his right mind as regards his intellect within.

These two great points of change have their distinct teachings.

As soon as the devils were cast out, the rescued demoniac became the recipient of charitable kindness from those around. From some of those who were present, he doubtless received what was sufficient to clothe his nakedness, and to supply the new need which had grown up.

Jesus had wrought, as was His custom, up to the immediate necessity of the case; and just as He commanded that meat should be given to the daughter of Jairus when He had raised her from the dead, but did not create any for the purpose; so here He allowed the demoniac to be clothed by the kindness of those who were around.

By this act they took him back into the fellowship of intelligent manhood; and it may be that, in leaving this part of the poor man's need to them, Jesus meant that there should be some teaching for ourselves. The torn garments of the Gadarene cast from him in his madness,—the raiment which, when he would use it, he received from the hands of kindly charity, have their teaching, as well as has that coat without seam, woven throughout from neck to foot, which God, for His own purposes, deemed worthy of being enshrined in prophecy; and which the Roman soldiers, for theirs, would not rend.

The view in which the rescued demoniac presents himself to us here is that of a recipient of charitable kindness.

Often, after the great work of Christ upon the soul, he who has experienced it needs much charitable help. It may be that this has its place in the deep providence of God. For while none but Jesus can do the great work, He wills that we, in our measure and place, should be fellow-workers together with Him.

When He raises Lazarus from the dead, He says, "Loose him, and let him go;" when He multiplies the bread, He delivers it to His disciples, and through them to the hungry crowd; when He will pay the tribute money, He sends Peter to cast a hook; when He will give them a multitude of fishes, they must cast at the right side of the ship.

In the work of our salvation—the great sacrifice upon the cross—Jesus stands alone; but in other things He is continually drawing His people into fellowship of work with Himself. It may be that, these are some of the bonds which are destined for ever to bind together that great family of which Jesus Himself is Head.

There is meaning in what the Lord leaves undone, as well as in what He does.

Often then, as we have said, immediately after Christ's great work, there is need of charitable help. The man upon whom He has wrought is alive to what he so recently was; he needs kindness, sympathy, the reception into fellowship, the covering over of that recent shame, at which, indeed, he is so much abashed himself.

It is we, such of us as are with Christ, who are to do this for him. We must not want to get him to sit at our feet. Alas! how many in a spirit of partisanship, or patronising, would do this. His place is at the feet of Jesus. But we are to accept and endorse that restoration of him to true manhood which Jesus has wrought.

The casting out of the old evil spirit leaves a man with many necessities; perhaps if we knew how many, we should try to supply him so far as in us lay.

This is one of the teachings suggested to us here. And as this comes to those who are with Christ, His followers and friends, when He does His great work, so the next comes to the person on whom such a work is wrought.

As soon as ever Jesus casts out the evil spirit, a new set of claims arise. The claims which the demons made were those of violence, and shame, and outragings of humanity in every form; the claims of the man's restored being were those of decency and order.

We are now only speaking of the demoniac in his external aspect. There is an outward decency, as well as an inward change, belonging to the spiritual life.

Would that it were always more enforced in preaching, more carried out in practice. This history of the demoniac speaks to two opposite sets of preachers—those who on the one hand urge the all-importance of an inward change, but tarrying there, take no heed to inculcate the necessity of a decidedly holy life; and those, on the other hand, who inculcate all holiness of outward living, but leave untouched the conversion of the heart.

Exorcised by Christ, and sitting clothed at His feet, we have, in a figure, the whole truth, without and within; and without because within, the blessed change is wrought.

The man did not complain of any irksomeness or hard restraint in wearing the unwonted raiment: so far from it, he would not have been contented without it; his condition of nakedness would have been uncomfortable, and out of harmony with his new life; for very shame's sake he would probably have rushed away to the tombs again, no longer, indeed, to delight himself in them, but there to be hidden.

But such an end would have ill-befitted this great work of Christ. The man's destiny was to be something very different from that; he was to sit clothed for awhile at Jesus' feet, and then to go forth clothed into the haunts of men, a robed preacher amongst his own kin of the wonder-working power of Christ.

Now what has been our experience? What do

we feel within ourselves? What aspect do we present to the world?

Is it possible that after Christ's great transformation of us, we can be content to feel as we used to do? Surely not. New cravings, new desires, new necessities, have sprung up. As the apostle's converts were his epistle, known and read of all men, so we must be the epistle of Christ's work, read and known of all. The world ought to be able to read Christians even externally. When the Gadarenes came to see what was done, they come to Jesus, and see him that was possessed with the devil, and had the legion, sitting and clothed, and in his right mind—the evidences of their senses shewed that he was a changed man. And that very evidence we should distinctly seek to give to the world. We must give them something to see. Whereinsoever we were known as bad, there let us seek to be known as changed. We may have many failures, but our very effort amid failures will be an undeniable testimony.

The external and the internal change were necessarily conjoined. They were so in the case of the prodigal—when he came to himself, (and in truth he had been beside himself,) before he returned, just as he was, with his shoeless feet and tattered rags, and his father brought forth the best robe, and put shoes on the way-worn feet.

The demoniac was now in his right mind—this clothing was with his full consent; he adopted it.

The Gadarenes recognised him as in his right mind, and in truth he was, and that much more than they knew—much more, indeed, if we push the matter to its furthest, than they were themselves.

Outward change was all they could understand, but that they saw. He himself had that which was peculiarly his own; he had received from Jesus something so individual and personal that, like the name in the white stone, none could know it save he who had received it; but there, in his own person, he furnished his countrymen with such evidence of change as they could receive.

We are bound to do the same. No one on earth ever knew, or could know the secret which was between that man's soul and Christ; but there was that in him which they who ran might read.

Christ wills that we should have secrets between us and Him. What love could there be without secrets?—secrets to be told, and to be heard—involving the delightful consciousness, that no one knows them but ourselves.

There will probably be such secrets even throughout eternity—secrets, if for no other reason, yet because they could not be put into words; they belong to that particular heart; and I can imagine its having a holy jealousy in parting with them; they are witnesses of the individuality of Christ's love with the individuality of ours—perhaps a witness of the personal bond by which we are held to Him.

The demoniac a resting man! ". When the Lord turned again the captivity of Zion, we were like them that dream" (Ps. cxxvi, 1); and so was it probably with this poor man. There he sat at the feet of Jesus, with, in all likelihood, no elaborate feelings, but just simply with consciousness of blessing and enjoyment of rest—a new one—a something, the like of which he had never felt before. No doubt if we set ourselves to seek for them, we should find the germs of all sorts of blessed feelings; but the one thing which probably filled his mind was the thankful consciousness of blessing. For well he knew that he had been unblest; it was but a very little while ago since he had been not only unblest himself, but one who hurt every one on whom he could lay his hands.

Now he had a quiet consciousness that he had entered upon a new phase of existence; and there was a great honouring of Jesus in that calm sitting at His feet.

There are many excellent people who despise, or at any rate do not make very much of a quiet consciousness—a calm enjoyment of Christ, like this.

They would drive the man about vehemently again. It is true they would do it with the best motives, but very effectually, nevertheless. They do not know the value of a quiet breathing-time at the feet of Jesus—that every moment there, is, in truth, a laying in of fresh energy, which will develop itself with power by-and-by.

But the demoniac could appreciate this rest; he had but to compare it with previous unrest; and bare rest, even with nothing else, was sweet. It had the charm of a new state, of new feelings; the tempest was over, and this was calm.

It was, indeed, something very new. The devil-possessed had known of but one acceptable rest, and he had cried aloud for it—it was to be let alone by Christ; but Jesus has another rest for him, it is at His feet. He knew of that, for him, which he could not know or guess of for himself, and He led him to it.

This is how the Lord acts. He hears us bid Him away in our madness, but triumphing over us, makes us love what we but a little time before both hated and dreaded—great closeness to Himself, a place at His very feet.

We do not suppose that there was anything speculative going on in that poor man's mind, that he had much thought at all; the sense of deliverance, of blessing, of what had happened to him, perhaps some vague sense of a relationship between himself and Christ, was all he had, but what an "all" was that!

We often misjudge, and make great mistakes about people who are not out in any open ministry or mission for Christ. We think they are bringing Him no glory and honour. In many cases it may be so, but assuredly not in all. The demoniac, as he sat there, was a glorious spectacle to men and

The Place of Rest.

angels; he was a witness to Christ's power; his satisfaction in being at those feet at rest was a great testimony to Christ's might. For here was displayed the triumph of the immaterial over the material. Material bonds never could have kept the man there, but immaterial did; human restraints, such as cords and chains, could do no more, but Jesus had done all.

Jesus, no doubt, could have restrained the brute force of the man, and caused him henceforth only to gnash his teeth in impotent fury amongst the tombs; but He went higher, He acted on the outward through the inward; He touched the fountain-head of the evil, and thus brought the afflicted one to tarry willingly at His feet.

In truth, there are many who will be held in by neither bit nor bridle, who will be bound neither with cords nor chains; but there is something stronger than all outward restraint. They know what they can resist, but they do not know what they cannot resist.*

---

* An interesting instance of this we have in the case of a man who came into contact with the excellent German pastor Weihe. "It was also confidently asserted, that all persons to whom Weihe gave his hand to salute them, were drawn into the magic circle, and that especially those who played the music (at weddings and gossipings) could never resist him. A musician of this class happening one day to hear such a thing, swore that Weihe should never get the better of *him*, and he would go to Gohfeld to try. His wife warned him of the danger, and begged of him not to venture; but in vain. He went to church, and determined

They have measured their strength with all that is outward, and been stronger than it all; now, if Jesus come indeed, they will be overcome. There may be tearing and rending, but the dealing with the inward will conquer.

Always believe that there is an 'inward' on which to deal—a something in man to which Christ, and he who goes in the name of Christ, can speak.

Jesus would not recognise this man as wholly devil; and no matter how much a man will, perhaps in reality, or perhaps in bravado, make him-

to sit in a part of it, where he thought the pastor was not likely to pass, so as to offer him his hand. But as he was unacquainted with the arrangements of this church, he posted himself just where the minister had to pass in his way to the pulpit; so that even before the service began, he had already got into danger. Weihe preached that morning with peculiar power and persuasive affectionateness; and at the conclusion of his sermon, he observed, 'It had been said of him that he could bring over people to his faith by merely giving them his hand. He wished he had such a power, for he felt so happy in the fellowship of Jesus Christ, that he was willing to go through the whole country, and from house to house, to reach out his hand to everybody, provided only he could thus win souls to the kingdom of God; but all he could do at present, was simply, as an ambassador for Christ, to beseech and exhort men, in Christ's stead, to be reconciled to God.' The musician was so touched by the powerful address of this good man, that he went home with his feelings quite changed; and as soon as he got there, he, without saying a word, took down the fiddle from the wall, and broke it in pieces, to his wife's terrified amazement. He now gave up his fiddling, became a bricklayer, and a sincerely pious man; and his wife followed his Christian example."—*Memoir of Rauschenbusch*, pp. 74-75.

self out devilish, he has, nevertheless, that which can be appealed to in the name of Christ.

Dr. Tholuck, the eminent theological professor and author, gave an address on the evening preceding his jubilee, in the hall of the Hotel Kronpriz, in Halle, before an audience consisting of a large number of pupils both old and young, and others, who had assembled with the doctor to celebrate the fiftieth anniversary of the beginning of his life work as a teacher. Speaking of those with whom he had had to do, he says, "There was another brought near to my heart by a godly mother. He soon fell among companions by whom he was led into the broad and slippery way. Contrition and return followed; but there came another fall. When he could be found at no other time, I sought him more than once at six o'clock in the morning. I visited him in prison, that I might remind him of what he well knew, but always forgot. A few days after, I said in my 'Hours of Devotion,' that the preacher would have a hard task, but for the witness even in frivolous hearts that says, '*He is right.*' The very next evening I received a note from him, 'Yes, now I know that God's Word has a witness in the human heart. I too have felt its working.' And he promised to abandon his associates and enter upon a new life. My words had brought him to himself; but would he have strength to stand fast?

Four or five days after, late in the evening, came

a card from him: 'Tholuck sighs, Tholuck prays; *but we will have our drunk out.*'

Yet this very man is now a preacher in Berlin. Only once have I had from him a reminder of the times gone by; but the recollection that lingers in my breast is warmer even than that reminder."

And this power of Christ to deal with what is altogether beyond our reach, must be our great hope—our hope as regards ourselves and others. It must be the mainstay of ministers in their dealings with souls; of teachers with their pupils; of parents with their children. It is from the heart there proceed all the evils which defile and disgrace a man; and it is spiritual influence alone which can get at the heart. Christ works from that which is within, to that which is without.

We have said that the demoniac had probably no elaborate or well-defined feelings while thus, during this brief period, at the feet of Jesus; just the consciousness and enjoyment of deliverance—calm, peace, quiet—these were the main ingredients of his happiness.

Let us not hurry new-born souls, by trying to force a multitude of well-defined, and, perhaps, advanced truths into their minds. In trying to give them more than they can take in, you may deprive them of what they have. Rest affords elements of growth.

And we may remark that, in the spiritual life it

is possible to commit an error in attempting to make every feeling or sensation take a particular and definite shape.

Some feelings are not destined to shape themselves for a season—some are, perhaps, never intended to do so. They are meant to be like diffused odours—like Æolian sounds. There is beauty and power, too, in the undefined things of God. Let us respect them; let us not be coarse and materialistic in meddling with them.

No doubt, there are men who would like never to have anything but a dreamy and undefined religion. They may be left with God to disabuse them of their error; but it is not because of that error that we should ignore this truth.

It is very possible that this man had some vague sense of relationship between Christ and himself; there was, at least, that of the healer and the healed; it possibly helped to bind him there to the feet, and we may be sure it energized him when he went to testify to those of his house.

Relationship to Christ!—let us establish that: and who can tell what it will do?

We must add a line upon the aspect of the once demoniac, as a satisfied man.

There are two interesting points in which he might be thus contemplated—as satisfied, though he had to part with an entire past; and though there lay before him an unknown future. Looked at in a mere natural point of view, these were calculated to be elements of disquiet; but we must view them from the stand-point of the work of Christ.

He who is acted on by Christ is willing to have the past a past indeed. He judges, he condemns it. He acknowledges that it was his—alas! too surely his; but now, at the feet of Jesus, he has to do with it no more. No fruit has he now in those things whereof he is ashamed; the time past suffices in which to have wrought such wickedness. He is not judged only of others, he has judged himself. The separation he wills to be complete; he wishes it to be an entire past. His only remembrance of it he desires to be with horror. He takes up the confession which says, "The remembrance of them is grievous."

Many persons cannot understand the willingness of Christ-acted-on men to part with a whole past—they urge as an objection to receiving Christ that they will have to give up so much; they say, how can I give up this or that; but such as have felt the power of Christ are satisfied—their will goes with His will.

There lay an unknown future before that man sitting so restingly and quiet at Jesus' feet; but it troubled him not; he sat and was at peace.

It may be that in after days he had to bear persecution, like the blind man whom the Jews reviled; in all probability he did not give that

The Place of Rest.

testimony which he was commissioned by Jesus to give, without some hazard to himself; but the future, all unknown and new as it must be, was nothing to him as he sat at the feet of Jesus.

Nor need it be to us. He who has parted with the past by the power of Christ, shall by that power be preserved in the future. The hand which has cut him off from a past of the evil ones, will bind him to a future of His own.

Therefore, dear reader, do not let the future trouble you with fears. You can meet with no enemy worse than the one over whom Jesus has already given you the victory. He sends you out into the future with great tokens, and earnests of His power. You have received no spirit of bondage, but a spirit of adoption, wherein you cry, saying, Abba, Father!

We need have no fears of that future into which we go at Jesus' command, and straight from sitting at His feet.

[The following recital, given by the Spanish martyr Matamoros himself to a friend of the writer of these pages, is, by her kind permission, here inserted. It seemed to the writer to embody so many points of resemblance to the demoniac, (his desperate character—the recognition of the manhood—the outcasting of the evil nature—the peace which followed; and that, even when the prospect of the future was dark—when he was about to be separated from the one to whom he owed all,) as to be an apt illustration of much which we have been considering in connection with the demoniac.

"It was during the spring time of the third year of my captivity," said Matamoros, "that my health seriously declined: often I was obliged to relinquish the attempt to walk across my cell; my weak state made it almost impossible to move. I thought, and my friends thought with me, that the time for my earthly tabernacle to be dissolved was at hand, and I rejoiced in the hope of going to my Saviour. The director of the prison, struck, no doubt, by the serious nature of my complaint, offered me, in the name of his chief, the permission to choose from amongst the other prisoners one who might be of service to me in the quality of a servant.

'Well,' said the officer, 'which of them will you have?'

I replied, '*Send me the most guilty of them all.*' There was in the prison a young man of about eight-and-twenty years of age, who was under sentence for several crimes, for two alone of which he was condemned to thirty-five years of hard labour. He had been the chief of a band of robbers, a man of savage energy and the most intrepid courage, who, on several occasions, had fought with the officers of justice commissioned to seize him, and in these encounters had always put them to flight. Such as he had been, he still remained in the prison: every one feared him, the officials as well as his companions, who often felt the effects of his brutal force. This was the man who was given to me as a servant. The director was evidently well pleased to separate him from the others. However that may have been, he was joyfully received by me. A feeling of deep compassion took possession of me on learning his history, as related by the jailor.

By degrees the respect which this unfortunate man shewed towards me began to be changed into affection. More than once he said to my mother, 'Ah, madam, if your son could be set at liberty by shutting up the jailors in his place in this dungeon, it should be quickly done! that would be easy work for me!' And I am persuaded that he would have put this design into execution, however perilous for himself, if I had not dissuaded him from it. On becoming better acquainted with his character and his tastes, I was convinced that notwithstanding his guilty and depraved life, he possessed a heart which was still susceptible of some generous and noble sentiments. One day he said to me, 'If I had not met with bad companions I would never have stolen; but persuaded by cowards who would not venture by themselves, and once entered upon their course, theft became habitual to me. However,' he added, with an expression of satisfaction, 'I have never taken anything from the poor, and neither has my gun or the point of my dagger ever shed a drop of blood. I was a robber certainly, but a robber who can boast of having been an honourable one!' Poor unhappy man! Some details of his history were completely unknown to every one. I was the sole person to whom he communicated them, for had they been known he could not possibly have escaped capital punishment. It was thus that little by little I was able to understand the inmost feeling of the man's heart. One morning, while I was preparing for my daily devotions, he was about to leave the cell. I begged of him to remain, and he sat down by my side. I opened the Bible at the third chapter of St. John. During the reading of it his face lit up with a bright expression, which seemed to increase every moment. On coming to verses 16, 17, 18, which I read slowly and with emphasis, a feeling of deep emotion appeared to overcome him. I understood that the moment was not to be lost, and I then read the eighth chapter of the Epistle to the Romans. We knelt down together, and it was given me to pray with fervour and confidence for this man, for whom I already felt an affection. My companion, on rising, shed a torrent of tears. I do not know that any other during my life-time had been as happy as that moment when I saw this soul enter upon the road to eternal life.

Leaving him under this blessed impression, it was afterwards I asked him, 'What do you think of the words we read—of what God Himself has said to us?'

'Ah, Don Manuel!' he replied, 'if I had known how to read I could have learned all these things, and I should not have been a criminal. Oh, it is very beautiful—I can never forget it. Ah, if I could but read I should not be so unhappy!'

'Well, will you learn to read? would you wish to begin?' was my inquiry.

'Yes, yes,' he exclaimed, with the greatest joy, and all the energy which characterised him; 'oh, yes, you are indeed a father to me! Oh, do this, and God will reward you for it.' I gave him the money to buy an A B C book, and the same day the book was in his pocket. We began at once, and from that time he seized on every opportunity to improve himself by asking assistance from those amongst the prisoners who knew how to read. It was in this manner that he employed a great part of the day. His progress was rapid, and at the end of six weeks he read tolerably well. He continued to listen to the Word of God, which I read every morning, and was present at several little fraternal and religious reunions which took place in the prison during the time of my imprisonment, evincing an inexpressible delight on these occasions. His peace of mind became from day to day more profound. He disquieted himself no more by seeking for means to regain his liberty, for he had arrived at a state of complete submission to the will of God. Our intercourse became more and more Christian and brotherly. I felt happy in the society of this man. His love extended itself to all the other prisoners, and he spoke to me of them with a profound interest; he knew their wants, and his greatest pleasure was to minister to their relief. Often have I seen him reading some portion of the New Testament to his companions. He used also to distribute some little tracts of mine; and I have no doubt that his conduct, at once prudent and firm, was productive of much good. As for me, I was strictly prevented from speaking to the rest of the prisoners; but he felt it a privilege to act as intermediary between me and them, by conveying some consolation or some religious book, which he gave with the words, 'Only look what Don Manuel sends you in the name of the Lord!'

So he went on, making each day some progress in the way to eternal life, while the sense of the increasing peace which he enjoyed became impressed upon his countenance. One day I received a visit from Mr. W. Greene, an English Christian, who has long interested himself in the evangelization of Spain, and one of the most zealous friends of the Spanish prisoners, who came into my prison to offer me the comfort of his fraternal affection. During the day he spent with me he had an opportunity of observing the behaviour of my servant, of whose life and circumstances he was informed by me. Deeply interested in the recital, Mr. Greene asked him, 'How can you bear the thought of passing thirty-five years in the galleys?' 'Ah, Sir,' replied my poor friend, 'what are some thirty years in the galleys to one who had been condemned to an eternity of punishment? Before I knew Don Manuel I thought of nothing but of making my escape, even if I should have shed blood in the attempt! I lived but in despair—but all that is changed; I know now that Jesus Christ came to save sinners—that by His deservings my sins are forgiven me—that my past life can no more be a cause of condemnation for me, for Jesus is *my Advocate.* This is why I go to the galleys tranquil and happy; for I feel assured of the salvation that Jesus has gained for me; and I rejoice at the prospect of His calling me to leave this life!'

The time at length arrived for my friend to leave the prison and go to the galleys. He wept abundantly on leaving me, yet he was able to say, 'My sorrow is exceedingly great at being separated from you! but let us comfort ourselves with the thought that He (Jesus) does not leave us, and that the love of God for us is immovable:—in His presence *we* shall meet again; shall we not?'

'*Yes*,' I answered; 'let us be faithful unto death, and we shall receive the crown of life!'"]

CHAPTER IX.

THE DEMONIAC.

(PART III.)
(THE MAN AS SEEN AT THE FEET OF JESUS.)

BEFORE we consider the subject of this man's being sent away from the feet of Jesus, where, as we should think, he might have so fitly been allowed to stay, it will be well worth our while to survey him as seen there by others—by the Gadarenes, his fellow-countrymen—those who had only too good right to know who he was; in whom, from very self interest's sake, the miracle wrought should have excited other feelings than those which it did.

As soon as tidings of what had occurred got abroad, all the people round about from city and country came together to Jesus. At His feet, they see the former demoniac sitting clothed and in his right mind; they are struck with awe; then they hear again how the wonder had come about, "and concerning the swine," and they pray Him to depart out of their coast.

They came to Jesus, and found *the man*.

What a sight! Man in the highest form—Jesus;

The Place of Rest.

man rescued from the lowest form—a habitation of devils—"the man who had the devils."

Here a great sight was presented to them; and we should have thought that the presentation of that picture—that first sight which struck their eye, ought to have produced an entirely different effect from what it did.

The Gadarenes were unconscious even of that which they might have known. The man now sitting quietly before them was the one who had been the terror of the neighbourhood. They had doubtless known plenty of instances of his violence—their wives and children probably trembled at the mention of his name; was it nothing that he should be made harmless, and that men could henceforth "pass by that way" which he had frequented and made unsafe? The boon even in this light was great—there they might read it, even in a single glance at Jesus' feet; but it does not seem to have come home—it was overborne by the destruction of the swine.

It is wonderful how slow men are to perceive, and to acknowledge, even the visible advantages which come from the working of Christ. They see men, who were the pest of the neighbourhood, becoming its blessing—those who set the worst example now setting the best—those who used by their idleness to be a burden to others, now industrious for themselves, and so on; and they will not see how good amongst them must be the presence of the One by whom such wonders are wrought. The world takes but little note of the great things it owes to Christ's working, in its anxiety to get rid of Christ Himself.

That they should be unconscious of the fulness of the wonder we need not be surprised. They could not, indeed, know how complete was the antagonism between Jesus and the devils; but the bare fact of His having power over them might have awakened some other thoughts than those which filled their hearts. But they did not; and we here see that what we think invincible, may often prove inoperative altogether.

We have been amazed that men could not be worked upon, as regards their own souls, when they saw and recognized the change wrought upon some neighbour, or in some member of their family; but that fear of loss, of having to give up, as they think, what they now value, counteracts it all. This is the power of material interest to hinder sight, or enquiry.

The Gadarenes found no swine, and this hindered their understanding or valuing what they did find. The wonder of the cured demoniac—that of the presence of One by whom such folk could be cured, could not compete with the value of the swine. That the devils had gone out of the man was more than counterbalanced by their having gone into the swine. They found "a man," where they had known only a habitation of devils, but they did not enter into that; they had not the spiritual wit to see and accept this great fact, and to refuse to put "a man" in competition with swine.

It is, indeed, amazing how low material interest will sink us—how it will make us forgetful of high charities; how it will so fill us with its own seen affairs, that we cannot interpret other seen things which are before our very eyes, in which, in truth, our deepest interests are concerned.

Wherever there is a great door open, there are the many adversaries; there is not a thing of earth but that has in it the capacity for interfering with the things of heaven—even when Jesus is most manifestly present, are to be found many swine.

Great loss is occasioned by lack of spiritual discernment. So is it here. These Gadarenes, if only they had been equal to the occasion, might have argued blessing for their own afflicted ones, or themselves, from the presence of Jesus. Had He cured such an one as the demoniac, then what might He not do for them and theirs! But they did not think of utilizing Jesus: they thought only of the swine; they knew not the time of their visitation.

Jesus, with the demoniac at His feet, was a proclamation to them that a Healer was in the midst of them for them and theirs; but they failed to hear it, and the opportunity passed away.

We need not be surprised. It is an awful thing to allow 'swine' to come into competition with

Jesus. The swine are always more or less present, and more or less attempting to do this; but when with full set purpose men give them the upper place, no marvel if Jesus move away.

And although it is hoped that the reader of these pages is one who prefers Jesus to all others, (else why has he taken up a book on such a subject as the "Feet of Jesus" at all,) still let him—yes, and let the writer, too, be on their guard against the intrusion of these swine.

We must not depress them into a position of no value, if we are to be taught by the story of the demoniac; for the swine were of price in the eyes of the Gadarenes.

The material things which come into competition with Christ, have their power from their value; and we must overcome that power by a high appreciative standard of who the Lord is, and what He does. We must say, 'such is Jesus, that all competition is forbidden.'

And from His gracious dealings with others, we must draw arguments for ourselves.

Has He received such and such an one? has He given a blessing to such another? what are these good things which He has scattered here and there, do they belong to the recipients of them alone? or have they nothing to say to me?

If I have spiritual discernment, they are all mine. For these men have not exhausted Jesus. It is true that virtue has gone out of Him, and He has perceived it; but what wills He but that more virtue still should flow from Him.

It is good, then, to see and note what Jesus has done—to understand it—to use it—to see those sights which may now be continually seen in the spiritual world—Jesus, and the man!

CHAPTER X.

THE DEMONIAC.

(PART IV.)
(THE MAN AS SENT AWAY FROM THE FEET OF JESUS.)

EVER in daily life, and in the experiences of our own souls, do we find it true that the Lord's ways are not as our ways, nor His thoughts as our thoughts. An example we find here. Jesus awfully taking the Gadarenes at their word, moved towards the ship which had brought Him to their shores. That ship had come full freighted with blessing; and now, with the exception of what might be left behind in and through the demoniac, it was about to bear all away again.

There was one, however, from among the Gadarenes, who willed not that Jesus should depart from those coasts, rather would he that Jesus should have tarried there for ever. Need we say that that man was the one so lately known as the demoniac. "And when he was come into the ship, he that had been possessed with the devil prayed Him that he might be with Him."

We can imagine the man's distress, perhaps his agony of mind, as he saw Jesus about to embark,

The Place of Rest.

and go whither he could not follow. As the boat receded from view, he at least would stand upon the shore, with his eye riveted upon it, until it faded from his sight. His eye would strain to secure the last glimpse of the One to whom he owed all; and as His figure became lost amid the others, and the boat itself became indistinct, and disappeared, he would return home disconsolate and alone.

Those who belonged to Jesus were about to embark with Him, and he who fain would be with Him too, must be separated from Him, to go and live amongst those who would none of his deliverer, and, it may be, of himself; for was it not partly through his cure that they lost their swine! To have sat at those feet, and now to see them depart, probably for ever from his shores—yes, to see them sent away, may have well grieved him to the very heart.

We need no great powers of imagination to picture to ourselves the feelings of this poor man as Jesus was about to depart. Love, reverence, gratitude, all the higher and nobler feelings of our nature, were probably putting forth their power in him who had so lately been a habitation of devils.

But other motives also may have had their place.

It was but a very little while before, and this man had been torn of the devils. His memory was charged with the pictures of what he had been. He shuddered at the thought; and also, it may be, at the dread lest those evil ones should find him again; and so entering into the house now swept and garnished, make his last estate worse than the first.

We cannot wonder if this poor man were full of fears. He thought, perhaps, of the wondrous look of Jesus' eye, and of the sound of His voice, as He commanded the evil spirits to leave him, and that he should not be safe away from that eye and voice.

If such thoughts filled his mind, they were natural, though not of necessity true. And it may be observed further that, the self-distrust which such a class of thought exhibits, is far more safe than that overweening confidence which, amongst many now-a-days is, on their first reception of the truth, so common.

If the poor man before us now had such a thought as we have been speaking of, it was in its measure a true one, for no one is safe out of the reach of the eye, and ear, and voice of Jesus. Only he knew no more than of the natural eye, and voice, and ear; and if so, no wonder if he were afraid to be left behind, far away from reach of them.

It is our happiness to know that we can ever keep within reach of the eye, and ear, and voice of Jesus; it is our safety to live in the power of this truth. It is well for us to keep steadily in sight the One by whom we have been delivered—

to have all our thought gathered in on Him—to expect that He who has acted against our enemies, will, if need be, do the like again.

The Church of God has this advantage over all who enjoyed the bodily presence for a season; Christ's people can ever be with Him, and He with them.

The man had a purpose for himself—he besought Jesus that he might be with Him; but Jesus had other purposes, and His and the man's were not the same.

No doubt he who has been acted upon strongly by Christ, becomes a man of purpose. New thoughts, and desires, and intentions fill his mind; he will do this and that, he will go here and there for Christ, but the Lord has often purposes for him other than his own.

And this is a lesson which we all need to learn, but more especially those who are just brought to Christ. The thought does not come to us naturally, we have to be shewn it by God.

It is not of necessity sin that we make purposes for ourselves, it is rather ignorance; we have come into a new sphere, where things are managed differently from what they were in the old one; and we know no better than to have our own yea, yea, and our own nay, nay, provided it be for God.

The witness of sincerity is very precious, but we must not content ourselves therewith, we must seek to know the mind of God, rather than our own. We must put ourselves at His disposal, and not think of disposing of ourselves.

For with all our sincerity we may go astray. We may take the wrong turning altogether, or enter on a path, which will not be the one in which He shall be most glorified.

Let us recognize the purposes of God. Let us say, He has His intentions for me, and let us seek to know them.

It may be that we shall have to learn them through our mistakes, but how much better to do so, through our obedience and self-surrender. God will bring His people to a knowledge of what He wills for them in some way; but the way may depend as to its bitterness or sweetness much upon ourselves.

Away from the feet! and Jesus to say it! Surely if ever man could be excused for thinking that Jesus made a mistake, this man might. If he went with Him, walking reverentially, with His apostles beside Him, or, it may be, even behind Him; if, when He tarried, he took up his recognized position at the feet of the One who had exorcised him, surely he would be a perpetual trophy of His might, an ever present witness of His mercy and power.

Would not human reason have said, 'it will be well for this man to be ever with Jesus, that men may look at him, and hear from himself and others what he had been, and so believe that Jesus came to overthrow the dominion of the devil.'

The Place of Rest.

Would it not be soothing and strengthening to Christ Himself amid the ingratitude of those He benefited, and the desertion of many who at hard sayings would drop off, and walk no more with Him, to have one, at least, who would ever sit at His feet, and look up with gratitude at His face, and drink in the sounds of His voice; and perhaps, for all we know, dare the soldiers of the Roman legion; and sit, with bowed head and weeping eyes, at the foot even of the very cross, preferring the feet of Jesus even there, at life's risk, to safety anywhere else.

So we should have thought, but such was not the mind of Christ. When He ascended up on high, He led captivity captive, but He carried about with Him no evidences of triumph, no soothing elements on earth. Those who accompanied Him were destined to be a trial, and not a comfort, in the day of His affliction, for they all forsook Him and fled.

But we ask ourselves the question as to whether any lack of tenderness can be discerned in Jesus, or any lack of appreciation, in thus sending this man from continual personal abiding with Him.

What Jesus did here, He did, as ever, wisely and in love. He destined that man to a higher mission than always sitting at His feet.

It may be that He who saw farther than any human eye, knew that the materiality of the position was not the best thing for that man's full blessing. At any rate it leads us to the thought that places of the greatest privilege, communion with particular persons, all of which we may deem to be essential to our spiritual happiness, or life, really are not so. In our spiritual life, what is, so to speak, material, may be too much *to* us, and too much *for* us. Whom not having seen, and whom not seeing, we love, is higher spiritual life than looking at the very body of Christ, and loving as we look.

We continually find ourselves clinging to the material in every possible form. Particular books, preachers, churches, companions, may become hindrances and not helps, because they themselves take the place of the spirit which belongs to them, wherein the true preciousness consists.

We often think it very hard that we are sent away from places of spiritual privilege; but God, who knows our material tendencies, orders it all in love.

It was when Jesus was on the very point of ascending, that He said, "Lo, I am with you alway, even unto the end of the world."

The materialistic may take a degraded form, as in the power of the swine to hinder the Gadarenes from receiving Christ; it may take a higher and more refined form, as in binding this man, as the only place of safety or of comfort, to the human body of the Lord.

As Jesus now sustains His church by His spirit,

and enables it ever by faith to see Him, and repose and rejoice in Him, though His bodily presence be removed; so, perhaps, He meant to sustain this Gadarene, and give him to be always with Him, even though His earthly form had taken ship, and was gone.

If only we have faith and spiritual understanding, we shall see that though outward presences depart, Jesus Himself is not to us, at least, really gone.

He then, who would be ever at the feet of Jesus, or companying with Him, is sent away. "Howbeit Jesus suffered him not, but saith unto him, Go home to thy friends, and tell them how great things the Lord hath done for thee, and hath had compassion on thee."

At first sight, when we hear Jesus not permitting this grateful man to follow Him, and shew his love and admiration by so doing, we may think that the Lord did not appreciate the offer; and that it was hard not to grant the request. But we find the denial accompanied with a command, which shews us that Jesus did not sever Himself from the man's offer of service, but accepted it, only in a different sphere from that which he himself had proposed. He would have been a disciple, but Jesus made him an apostle to the Gadarenes. The once demoniac received a commission from the Lord; he was left on His behalf a witness for

Him in the land where He had been rejected; the only human means through which anything could now be done for the people in those parts. All that could be known of His mercy and love, Jesus entrusted to that man.

In truth, the man who had the devils now received a high commission from the Lord—one which would require as much spiritual strength from above to fulfil, as it needed strength from beneath to be what he had been before.

He was appointed to solitary testimony amid an exasperated people, and those, his own countrymen. He had aimed high when wishing to be always with Jesus—and he is placed high by Jesus.

Though the Lord was going away, the connection between the Gadarene and Himself was not to be severed. The former demoniac was to be appointed to a place of singular honour and responsibility—to that of solitary testimony. He, and he alone, was to be Christ's witness amongst his countrymen.

Some might say—Is this all? but what a 'this' is it! What a trust is it, and what a man to have it reposed in! The place of solitary witness is one from which flesh and blood might well shrink, but it is one of great honour in the sight of God. Jesus does not reject the service of the Gadarene; He only orders it in a different channel from that which he proposed.

The former demoniac was ready to give up home to follow Christ; and herein, perhaps, Jesus found a special suitability for His ministry at home.

It is often the one who is prepared to sacrifice home itself for Jesus, who is privileged to do most there. It many a time needs a spirit of devotion to do anything amongst our own friends—it is sometimes easier to go to the heathen than to them. They, perhaps, can taunt us with what they have known us to be—they can say, "thou wast altogether born in sins, and dost thou teach us?" we may rest assured that there is ample room for the exercise of the most devoted spirit in home.

That Gadarene might have suffered as much despite from his countrymen, as the apostles who took ship with Jesus ever did in their more extended field of testimony and labour.

The Lord appears to have recognised here, in this renewed man, a true relationship to his own friends and people. The demoniacal possession had disturbed it; but now that was removed; and being lifted up into a position altogether superior to anything he could ever have had simply as a Gadarene, he must, in this new sphere, recognise the old relationship, and witness to his friends and relatives of Christ.

There is a peculiar power in the witness of a changed man in his own home, where he, and all about him, is well known. There are diversities of testimony—there is that of the man who, to all outward appearance, has lived blamelessly, and that of him who has been turned from the error of his way—that of a John, who leaned on the bosom of Jesus, and of a Paul, who persecuted Him.

Whatever power there was in the changed circumstances of this man, Jesus will have him exercise amongst his friends.

The Lord sends him back to the place from which he had specially fled. Thither, whence he had been driven forth by the influence of the devils, is he returned by the influence of Christ.

The man was to be restored to the highest instincts of humanity, not merely to companying with Jesus, but to doing good in the name of Jesus.

Perhaps it was needful that this man, who had fled from home and friends, must be returned to both, as a testimony to the completeness of the undoing of the devils' work by Jesus.

Jesus did not take the Gadarene away, because there were still the mountains, and caves, and tombs, and the stones wherewith he cut his flesh, all remaining where they used to be during the time of his possession by the devils; they remained as they were, but the once demoniac was changed as regards them. He had a mission to his friends —one which would occupy all his powers and energies, in which he could spend all his strength.

We are reminded of how it often is with ourselves. We are obliged to live amid the scenes of

The Place of Rest.

old trials and temptations, ever recalling to our memory what we have been—sometimes we have to live amongst them, and hear them inviting us to be with them as we were before.

But their attraction, and power, and spell are broken. They no longer fit the heart on which Jesus has wrought—that to which they could appeal has gone; they are, and ever must be, the same, but we are wholly changed.

And now let the reader gather for himself some teaching from what has been brought before him. To each one upon whom Christ has wrought there is a sphere. It may not be—it probably is not, the one which self would choose, but to Him let us leave the ordering of His own interests; and how we are best to give testimony to His glory.

Let no man despise or neglect his sphere, because it is that of home. Some of the highest victories of the cross have been won in home; some of the greatest testimony given to Christ has been there.

And should the reader of these lines be appointed to a place of lone testimony amongst his earthly friends, when he would fain be always with the people of the Lord, let him remember the honour and responsibility of his position.

The Gadarene was left in that land where Jesus was not received, as in a measure the representative of Jesus Himself. He—rescued, changed, a friend where he had been a foe, was the counteractive to the hard thoughts which may have kept possession of his countrymen's minds because of the loss of their swine.

Strange it may seem that Judas the traitor should be allowed ever to company with the Lord, and that this man, who longed to be with Him, who would, to all appearance, have been a faithful and energetic disciple, is not allowed, as he so earnestly wished, to be with Him. But it teaches us an important lesson. It shews us how little we can argue from external privileges and positions.

Jesus takes ship and goes away—and the Gadarene returns to give testimony amongst his friends. We hear no more of him; but we may well believe that when the last glimpse of the ship was lost, and he turned his steps home to fulfil the mission with which he had been entrusted, he went in the strength of the Lord, and the remembrance of the power and love by which he had been brought, clothed, and in his right mind, to sit at the 'feet of Jesus.'

CHAPTER XI.

THE FEET OF JESUS, THE PLACE OF PERSONAL SUFFERING.

"They pierced my hands and my feet:" Ps. xxii, 16.

THIS Psalm in its almost every letter is so associated with the particular points of our blessed Lord's suffering upon the cross that we feel a kind of jealousy as to the least change in the well known words.

Happily the criticism which appears to necessitate an alteration in the very passage which stands at the head of this chapter, does not really rob us of any old familiar thought, or more important still, of a great and precious fact.

Hengstenberg translates this verse, "For dogs compass me, the band of the wicked besets me, like lions on my hands and feet."

Ainsworth translates it, "They lion-like pierced my hands and my feet." And he appends this note. The original hath a double reading, *Caari*, (like a lion,) and *Caru*, (they digged or pierced.) This latter, the Greek followeth; but the Chaldee in the Masorite title keepeth both readings, "they did bite like a lion." Scott says, "The clause indeed rendered, 'They *pierced* my hands and my feet,' stands in the original at present, '*As a lion* my hands and my feet.' But this contains no clear sense at all. A very trivial change gives the reading of our version. The Septuagint, which is certainly more ancient than the Christian era, renders it as we do, and there seems scarcely the shadow of a doubt, but this is the genuine reading, though the general exactness of the Jews in preserving their Scriptures, precludes the charge of an intentional alteration."

We are not concerned at the change which seems to be required, for it detracts nothing from the great fact of the piercing, or of its being foretold. It only embodies in imagery the same great fact, suggesting to our minds the activity of the ferocity with which the wounds were inflicted on the hands and feet of Jesus.

Our subject shall be—

THE FEET OF JESUS THE PLACE OF PERSONAL SUFFERING.

The lions have indeed come about Him, they have come into contact with Him; they have done so, in the only way which we could expect them to do; they have torn Him; the nail is driven through His feet, even as it is through His hands; the marks of the wild beast's claws are in both hands and feet; the nails are no mere pieces of iron, but the envenomed fangs of active foes.

Here then we have Jesus in pain, in acute personal suffering, from the piercing and wounding of hands and feet.

We must first pause upon the picture of Christ in pain.

Now, when we come to speak of pain at all, we enter upon profound mystery. The problem of the existence of pain is perhaps one of the most difficult which can be submitted to us for solution. Why should there be pain? why should Jesus the Son of God have suffered it?

We are told that in the far off history of this world there was pain.* "The leaves of the stone book of geology have written on them not merely records of death, but likewise of pain. The fossil fishes which abound in many of our strata, are not found stretched out in the postures of repose, which they would have assumed had they perished calmly; but like men who die in battle, with agony upon them, their bodies are thrown into violent contortions." "Historically," says the same writer, "pain is ingrained and inseparably interwoven into the whole fabric of our system."

There is little use in our speculating as to the origin of pain; just as little as in our speculating on the origin of evil; or as to whether the one and the other were always inseparably connected. Nor is there any use in our following out the idea as to whether Jesus had in these prehistoric times a connection with suffering; and what that connec-

* Wilson's Religio Chemici.

tion was. It is not given to us to know these things. Enough for us to call to mind that the very first mention of the Lord is in connection with suffering—His heel is being bruised.

The first promise then connects Jesus with pain. It leaves the problem of evil, and of pain as in connection with it, unsolved, but it connects Him with it. He is not represented as the unscathed destroyer of pain—as the One, who from the power of stamping on the head of His foe can escape unhurt himself; but as an endurer—a wounded victor, hurt, and that sorely, in the conflict in which He overcomes His foe.

Christ then is *in* this great problem of pain—in the midst of it. He has drunk the cup of suffering to the dregs; He has partaken largely of such suffering as falls to the lot of man in the flesh; He who knows all about pain, what it is—what part it plays in the great arena of God's glory—what are its uses—what its mysteries, has let it come upon Him Himself, and enter His human nature, and do all that it can do against Him.

Now here, the feet of Jesus, be they torn as with a lion's claws, or pierced as they were by the nails upon the cross, come very helpfully to me.

This great problem of pain oppresses me when I think of it, when I feel it. 'Why am I thus?' is a question which many a sufferer may put to himself; and as he cannot answer, dark thoughts cross his mind.

Place of Personal Suffering.

Jesus' disciples ask Him, "Master, who did sin, this man, or his parents, that he was born blind?" and Jesus answers, "Neither hath this man sinned, nor his parents, but that the works of God, should be made manifest in him."

Lazarus' sickness, with its temporary death, and the sufferings whatever they were which were endured, were for the glory of God, that the Son of God might be glorified thereby.

There were plenty of others lying dead, upon whom, as we should have thought, resurrection power might have been shown, without Lazarus, a living man, being made to suffer and to die; but we are told of this particular case that, it was "for the glory of God."

But why? why cannot He be glorified without suffering? Ah, there is the problem—and we have no means whatever of even guessing at a solution.

But the pain presses—the pain of others—our own. I am practically in the problem; then all that I can do is to say, 'And so was Christ.' I look at Him in His life sufferings, I see Him on the cross, lion-like enemies besetting His hands and feet during life; and lion-like claws fixed in those nailed feet at His death, and I say, "As He was, so are we in this world."

Pain is in itself sinless; Jesus took it on Himself, therefore it cannot separate me from God. He said, "The cup which my Father hath given me, shall I not drink it?" Therefore in suffering this, whatever it may be, I am in sympathy with the mind of God; my spirit and my body stagger at being in this place, and under these circumstances of trial, but I am where Christ was, and therefore though I suffer, I need not fear; the working out of the problem of my present suffering is in the hand of God.

When the feet of Jesus were nailed to the cross, He left all with His Father. He left it thus, as He said, "Father into thy hands I commend my spirit;" even so, we must, if need be, simply suffer, pierced through, yet saying 'Father.'

Vast and overwhelming as is this problem of suffering, let us remember that, although we cannot grasp its great circumference, we can be sure of one or two matters of immense importance to ourselves.

One is, that there may be great dignity in suffering; another, that we individually may emerge well, indeed be immense gainers out of it; and a third, that Christ is linked to us in it; those pierced feet bind Him to all the piercings of humanity; and, if we might so express ourselves, hold Him in that position.

And all this is, because so it was with the suffering and piercing of our Lord. We are in fellowship with Him in the mystery of pain.

Thus much in part do we learn from Christ's feet being pierced with those cruel nails, and suffering physical pain.

Now let us consider,

THE FEET AS THE MEANS OF ESCAPE.

Here we have first of all, the means of escape willingly allowed to be cut off. Jesus knew full well, when He went forth into the garden, that His enemies would come thither, that there was one who knew the place, and who would make a fatal use of that knowledge.

It was night, and there was every possibility of escape; for the feet which took Jesus to the place of betrayal, might have taken Him from it.

And for aught we know, it may have been a part of the trial of our Lord, to feel that moment after moment was passing, each one lessening the opportunities for escape; that He could go, but that those feet must tarry until he came, whose kiss would conduct them to the cross. The feet of Jesus tarried in that garden, not because flesh and blood would not have desired in themselves to have had them bear Him far away, but because in perfect obedience He was not only to endure suffering when it came, but to await it while it was coming.

And when at last Jesus hung upon the cross, with hands and feet both transfixed; what was He but a spectacle of utter helplessness—the means of defence and of escape both gone?

Surely, there is something very teaching to us in this yielding of Himself by Christ to God. How few of us have arrived at that state of subjugation of self which makes one willing to forego struggling—to await the on coming of the dispensation—to accept the helplessness of the dispensation when it comes. We need every help to enable us to do this; let us accept this one, of a contemplation of Jesus' feet nailed and pierced. Those feet were in their very helplessness, at that time, the embodyment of an amazing will; and have we ever thought that, an amazing will for oneness with the mind of God may be found in our simple readiness to see means of escape fail and come to nought.

The feet tarrying in Gethsemane and fixed to the Cross, are the same; and the preliminaries of our sorrows, and our sorrows themselves, should be pervaded by the one spirit also.

The position of helplessness is *willingly* taken up. The time had come for it. Jesus had on previous occasions escaped from His enemies, but now the hour had come, and with it the will was ready also. Jesus accepts the position of helplessness.

Now, there is a great difference between what is enforced, being borne simply as such; and that which is accepted—entered into; and so, in point of fact, made our own. And there was this very difference between the sufferings of Jesus and ours. We too often bear, only because we cannot help it; we, as the saying is, make a virtue of necessity, our will is not in our trial.

Place of Personal Suffering. 161

It may be that, we do not think much of the helplessness which it was the will of Jesus to assume for us; how He thirsted and could not get water at the well of Sychar without human help; how He hung upon the cross, nailed hand and foot and could not stir.

Surely Jesus as He thus hung was in this respect, as in many others, a representative man. His people were destined often to be brought into positions of utter helplessness, which they were to accept as fulfilling the will of God; and they could, if they had only marked the feet nailed to the cross, look back on Jesus hanging there, and in that sight find strength and endurance, and more than resignation, even entire conformity with the Father's mind. When the executioner drove those nails through the feet of Jesus, He wrote many homilies for the church of God—yes, even a page of revelation without knowing it.

Helplessness has trials peculiarly its own. It is a specially humbling condition. It is one into which God has frequently called His people. Jeremiah, Job, Ezekiel in symbolic vision, Daniel, Paul, all had trials of it; and few children of God there are who cannot look back, and see times of helplessness in their past lives.

Perhaps we dread such in the future; we think, 'this my comfort and stay will leave me,' or, 'this means of earning my bread will be taken from me;' or, 'I shall be put into such circumstances

M

that I shall be hedged in; and enclosed with hewn stone, (Lam. iii, 9,) and we fear that our old energies will be gone and we cannot resist, or stand up as we used to do against such things. We shall be nailed, and cannot stir. The cross will enable us to meet all such thoughts, if we know how to use the sight which we see there. The feet, afterwards free with such a liberty as was never known by mortal man, are now nailed; and as with Jesus so with us; 'tis but a little while, and God will deliver us, for He will have us; and will set us, as He set Jesus in a large room.

There was something peculiarly galling to Jesus in remaining thus nailed helplessly to the cross. For He knew He had the power to escape. "If Thou be the Son of God come down from the cross," had in it an element of bitterness which the human nature of Jesus must have felt. For He could have come down. He had the power to escape, but there was a higher power of love to God and man which forbad the using it. Only that could not be revealed to those who were around; so there He hung, His acceptance of that fixing by the nails a. bearing of the imputation of being an impostor; for if He came down the Jews said that they would believe.

It was a part of our blessed Saviour's trial that He had to allow Himself to be misunderstood; that when the Jews cried, "If thou be the Son of God, come down from the cross," He should abstain

Place of Personal Suffering. 163

from coming, and let them, in their wilful blindness, believe Him to be an ordinary man.

There is a morbid glorying in being misunderstood. Some people bear this trial in the power of bad influences, and comfort themselves all the while with the thought of their great virtue in quietly bearing to be so ill-used. They have a spiteful pleasure in the thought that so-and-so is wrong in his opinion, and would not correct him, but would rather that he continued wrong. And so their principle of endurance is one of self-satisfaction and self-exaltation—all the more dangerous because so inwardly hidden.

And it is wonderful how far such a state of feeling will carry a man—how much it will enable him to bear—how much it will take the bitterness out of being misunderstood.

But how was it with Jesus? He had already given His proofs; He had told and shewn them what He was; this last proof He could not give them, unless at the loss of a world's salvation, and so He had to bear the imputation of being no Saviour at all. This being misunderstood was, no doubt, one of the elements of the bitterness of the cross.

It is true, Christ knew that the righting time would come, but the present was the present to Him for all that—it must have been if His humanity were true.

Patiently to allow ourselves to be misunderstood,

when we cannot clear ourselves except at a cost which is not lawful, is Christ-like indeed. "Come down," they said; and had the pierced feet moved at their call, how could we have been saved? But the pierced feet stay still; and a voice comes to us from the foot of the cross, saying, 'Be thou still also.' Deep pity there doubtless was in the heart of Jesus for those by whom He was misunderstood —pity was what He felt, and not self-satisfaction, or hate—the very pity made it the harder to bear. So perhaps it may be with all misunderstandings from which we suffer, but God will provide a clearing time; and let that suffice.

Jesus had to veil His power upon the cross. He held that power, not for self-aggrandisement, or self-vindication, or self-deliverance, but for His Father's will; and He had to hear its existence called into question, and yet give no reply. That which was His own, it was His pleasure to consider as in trust; and the carrying out of the trust involved humiliation. "He saved others, himself he cannot save."

A very important teaching flows from this for our daily Christian life. We have much, which, speaking of things in an ordinary way, we say is our own. How far have we attained to the idea of 'our own being in trust'—of our holding it as such? The motionless, pierced feet of Jesus, by the fact of their being motionless, teach us this lesson of power in trust. So, then, it is not because

I can do this or that, or have the right to do it, that I can choose to do so. If I have given all to God, I hold all in trust from God, and for Him. It is a blessed experience when we will to hold in trust, that, which, speaking in the ordinary sense of words, we might say is our own.

It was an element of Christ's power over Himself, that He knew He had to subordinate all to a purpose—this was one of the human elements of His power. "Wist ye not that I must be about my Father's business," was the motto of His life, and also of His death. He had a baptism to be baptised with, He had a will to fulfil; and power and everything else were subordinated to this.

To a like source may be traced the success of many a man in life; if his pursuit has been that of honour, or wealth, or scientific investigation, if he has subordinated everything to it, he has generally succeeded. There is one sense in which it is good to be a man of one idea. St. Paul said, "This one thing I do."

In Christ's human character the power of purpose held a place—it wrought to its legitimate end. We do not say that Christ was only human—we say distinctly that He was more than human; but we say with equal distinctness that the human was not lost in the divine; and He calls upon us, in our low, fallen type of humanity, to rise under the example of His high humanity, and be people of purpose—subordinates to purpose—aye, and successful in purpose. That was what Saint Paul was, when he says, in 1 Cor. ix, 27, that he kept his body under, and brought it into subjection—that is what we have not been, and therefore why we have so often failed.

See in the pierced feet remaining motionless on the cross—the power of purpose.

Recognize also in the One hanging helplessly there, the Man of power in Himself—the One stronger than all who were around. The pierced feet could—but would not. And no one saw this. The secret was with Christ Himself alone.

We do not see all the strong men in the spiritual world—in all probability very few of them. God's strong ones are often hidden ones. Out of the mouth of babes and sucklings He ordaineth strength.

Perhaps one of the greatest displays of strength that Jesus ever really made, (though man recognized it not) was when He refused to answer the mocking taunt, and disengage the pierced feet from the cross; and who can tell where displays, far less in their degree, but like in kind, are now being made! And we may make them. We may be the strong men of God in our circumstances of weakness, in our times of piercings—down-trodden by the world, and in its estimation; strong ones by the grace of God, and before God.

There are times when the people of God are put in a position somewhat like Christ's; when they could speak, but their tongue is tied—when they could do, but they must not stir—when they could extricate themselves from some unpleasantness, but they must bear it. No one knows the secret of our reticence but ourselves; and so, no one can administer any comfort to us in what we are enduring, or can help us to hold out. But we are not without a Helper, and a sympathizer too. Jesus knows all about these positions; He presents Himself before us with His feet nailed to the cross. He is taunted, He is called upon to come down; but He stirs not, He endures. He accepts the peculiar bitterness belonging to the situation; and He says to us 'In all your afflictions I was afflicted, and have suffered in all points like you, only without sin.'

But this position has another side. All sufferings have another beside that which is at first presented to the view in the aspect of bare endurance.

This position of helplessness was one of peculiar nobility. It was one in which Christ could and did exercise great mastery over 'self'—over what would have been the impulses of mere human nature.

Power rightly used is always noble; and Christ used His to remain where, and as, He was. There was perfect mastery over 'self.'

Now, it is in this way that we are to look at positions of stillness. We are not to fret ourselves about, or lament over, their apparent feebleness;

they are really altogether above what they seem. And it is by this thought that we are to comfort, and strengthen, and calm ourselves, in all our trial times, when the trial assumes this form. God wills us to have perceptive power for true honour—for that which lies underneath the outward husk and show of things—for that which is so in His eyes. And we may be sure the true honour is to be found in all positions in which He places us; many a bed is a greater place of power than a throne, for the one who lies helpless there has mastery over will.

The pierced feet were to all human appearance in a place of weakness, they are in reality in that of power; and so it may be with us. Let us see what underlies our position when we are pierced and helpless; and we shall often become not only contented, but even satisfied with our lot.

This piercing was a *part* of a great accomplishment. It was not a final position, and Jesus knew this well. It was a part of a great whole; and Jesus put it in its proper place. He knew that for a few hours the feet must be pierced; and terrible as that piercing was, He appropriated to it its own place, but no more.

And this is the very way in which we are to deal with our piercings, however bitter they may be at the time. They are not final. They do not form a perfect circle in themselves. They are but a part of a great whole; and that great whole means

Place of Personal Suffering. 169

glory to God, and profit and comfort and everything good to ourselves.

Jesus knew that for a little while His pierced feet were in the appointed place; but that yet a little while, and they would come forth from the grave, and ascend from the mount; and that beneath those feet His enemies should be subdued, and become His footstool.

When we allow our sufferings to assume an aspect of finality, and completeness in themselves, we give them a power over us which is not according to the ordinance of God. We put more into the suffering than He ever intended to be there. We throw it out of gear; and looking at it by itself, and as unconnected with other things, we become depressed and confused, and often take up altogether a wrong train of thought with reference to it.

We are living in a fragment in every possible way—in a fragment of time—in a fragment of revelation—in one of experience; and if we persist in making a part the whole, we must go altogether astray.

Jesus, we can well believe, assigned to the piercing of His feet its proper place as a part of the great accomplishment; and let us try to connect our individual sorrows with a great whole. No doubt we have the disadvantage of being ignorant of what the whole is; but we need not be troubled about that. It is in the main God's glory, and our truest and largest good—good, for the bringing about of which it may be that these sufferings were absolutely necessary, though we know not why.

And thus the cross connects itself in an unexpected way with our daily life; not only as regards the great sacrifice hanging thereon, but as regards the incidentals of that sacrifice also. Those pierced feet are in connection with sofas and beds, and reduced means, and imprisonments of many a kind. There are lines of union drawn between them all and the cross—every one of our piercings has a counterpart in those of Christ.

And especially if we be acting nobly, in intelligent appreciation of God's will and glory in our trial. For all noble things lead up to the cross. They turn to that, as plants in a dark place to the light; they rise thither as incense when set free by fire, ascends in perfumed clouds; towards the sky.

There is great strength and uplifting from the consciousness of sympathy with Jesus. We may, if we use the words aright, say 'His head and ours,' 'His hands and ours,' 'His feet and ours.'

Yes! these may be one in the performance of God's will, in sympathy with the Divine mind. We may go through all our sufferings in this oneness with our Lord, seeing deeper than the world sees, and fulfilling a mission which not only the world, but, perhaps, even our nearest and dearest friends may not understand.

Let us note too the position of those feet in relation to the enemies of Christ.

His foes thought they had so pinned them to the accursed tree as to bar all future progress. Little did they know their future destiny, the progress which they were to make because they took up this position on the cross. They did not know that they would ascend on high; that they would return in power, and stand on Olivet. The pierced feet had a mission as pierced which they never could have had otherwise; the cross is their starting point. And whither do they travel now? Let us rather ask whither do they not? It is with pierced feet that Jesus comes to me now; it is with pierced feet He leads me; and the leadings and the visitings of pierced feet are very precious.

It may be that in the hot sunshine of the world we seek such leadings but little, and but little care for such visitings; it is not pierced feet we wish to see crossing our threshold, we are not in sympathy with them; but when the glare is subdued, when we are so wrought upon by the Spirit's mellowing influences as to be willing to receive Jesus as He really is, as God sets Him forth, and not as we would have Him, then we rejoice to see the piercings of the feet.

For when Christ with such feet leads on before, we are willing to follow after. We say, 'Here is one skilled in all of suffering. Here is one experienced in personal trial. He will lead softly, and surely, and tenderly. He will not set the pierced foot down too roughly. And when He comes to me, how gently, how meekly, albeit He is the Lord of glory, will He enter into my house!'

There will be none of the roughness of mere human authority about Him, no heavy tread, no tramp as of an armed man, but the soft step of a pierced foot.

There are many, alas! how many houses, the threshold of which Jesus would not have been allowed to pass with pierced feet. These would mind the dwellers therein too much of the claims of the suffering One; beside which, they have enough in the world; they have no sympathy with a suffering One, they neither want Him to understand them, nor do they want to understand Him.

They think that the on leadings of the One with pierced feet can only be into piercings for themselves, that He has no paths but those of sorrow, or gloom; but the pierced feet can tread in very pleasant places; they know the way to paths of peace—they cross streams which sparkle, and meadows which flower, and heights from which distant views can be obtained; they know the cool places of the valleys; and here, as well as on rough hard stones, they often lead, and then such places are safe; when the feet of Jesus go before, we can have no hurt.

We may here note how the pierced feet help to

present us with a view of the perfection of the suffering of Christ.

His whole man—His person from head to foot is marked as it were with these piercings—the head—one extremity is crowned with thorns; the feet, the other extremity, are pierced with nails. And at either we find the sounds of mockery. Pilate inscribes over the crown of thorns 'The King of the Jews;' the Jews themselves mock at His feet, saying, "If thou be the Son of God, come down from the cross."

Is this without any meaning for us? Surely a Christ, perfect as it were from head to foot in suffering, must be especially precious to us who have so many sorrows, and of such various kinds.

Nowhere can trouble come upon us, but that He is prepared with experimental sympathy. The head, the hands, the side, the feet, are all pierced. The whole man bears the marks of woe.

In our many sorrows, let us look at that, His completeness of suffering. Suffer when we may, let us turn to Him, and there shall we find that He suffered also; so that let the spear, or the thorn, or the nails, touch us where it will, we shall be able to say, 'I am sympathized with, and understood.'

THE FEET WHICH HAD GONE ABOUT DOING GOOD.

When Peter opened his mouth to teach Cornelius and those who were with him, he spoke of Jesus of Nazareth, as the 'One anointed with the Holy Ghost and with power,' as One who went about doing good, and healing all that were oppressed of the devil, for God was with him. Acts x, 38.

How full that good was we can see from Matt. iv, 23, where we are told that, "Jesus went about all Galilee teaching in their synagogues, and preaching the Gospel of the kingdom, and healing all manner of sickness, and all manner of disease among the people." Thus, and thus only were the feet of Jesus occupied on earth. In this work they went on long travel—in this they were weary, dust-stained, and unrefreshed; if the history of each foot-fall could be written, it would contain some portion of the story of His love to man.

And yet these are the feet of which we read here, as pierced and torn—these are the feet which men nailed to the cross. The ingratitude which they showed would be in itself enough to furnish subject matter for long sad thought. And with the ingratitude, the folly, and the madness. For were they not there recklessly shutting up the means of their choicest blessing; forbidding all other journeys for good; saying that no more should the feet of the Healer travel through their land to the home of the sick, and the tombs of the dead; no more should those of the teacher go through coast and village, and into temple and synagogues bearing God's last and greatest message to their kind.

They crowned with thorns the head which had never thought of them but for good; and they pierced the heart which had never felt towards them but love; and they nailed the hands which had fed and healed them; and the feet, which had journeyed only to carry blessing hither and thither throughout their land.

Sin is indeed a guilty madness, and nowhere is it more plainly seen so than here, when man nails his best benefactor to a cross.

But let us turn our attention to one or two other thoughts, from which we get important teaching for ourselves.

And first of all we observe that this great injury is suffered in the very instrument of blessing to man.

Now this is in itself enough to raise some questionings within our hearts.

Why did not the goodness of Jesus protect Him from this indignity and suffering, and this summary ending to His mission of doing good?

Jesus came into the world as it was from its first days of sin—from the time of the murdered Abel, when goodness attracted instead of repelling injury. He was in the world, not as He would have made it, but as it was; and it was to act on

Him as coming to the laws of evil; and the laws of evil were that, such as He were not worthy to live. Now this comes home practically to many of the children of God, and all the more so, the more like they are to Christ.

God's people often allow themselves in very mistaken ideas, with regard to their position in the world.

They expect to be appreciated, to be valued; that for their very usefulness and the good they do, they will find help and not hindrance, honour and not shame. They are vexed at the injustice and the stupidity of those with whom they have to do, in not recognizing the value of their work.

Let them look at the cross; at the head and hands, and feet, which are all pierced there; and when they have looked, say, 'the disciple is not above his master.' They are placed in their trial in this respect in oneness with their Lord. Their piercings have this characteristic in common with His.

But we sometimes have thoughts in this matter connected with God Himself. Sometimes in folly, sometimes in bewilderment, sometimes in ignorance, we think when we see health, and property, and position, which were used for advancing good, taken away; and illness, and loss, and depression in the social scale taking their place, that this ought not to be. We think that all such blessings and opportunities should be spared; in a word, that no cross should be laid on them.

Here is a man who spent the bulk of what he had in doing good; and now, in a moment, it is taken from him. Violence has come on his property, so far as doing good goes, he is nailed hand and foot. Barabbas gets off scot free, but the man of God is practically crucified with his Lord.

The staggering of David comes upon us; and we have need to go into the sanctuary of the Lord to understand this.

Into that sanctuary Jesus doubtless went. Amid the many thoughts which flooded His mind as He hung upon the accursed tree, these, perhaps, may have had place. When the last breath was parting, Jesus cried with a loud voice, "Father, into Thy hands I commend my spirit," but who can tell what He had been committing as He hung there; how many thoughts like these passed in sorrow through His mind, or into the light of the sanctuary in which He dwelt.

They may have been projected on His mind as being darts of the evil one, or they may have risen as the sorrowful and sinless thoughts of One who felt that all things were out of course; but if indeed they crossed the Saviour's mind in that dark hour, there fell upon them, we may be sure, sanctuary light; and in that light, He saw light.

We may rest assured that there is a solution to all dark dispensations of this kind; they are the mysteries of God; but He who allows them to enter into His plans, can unravel them if He see fit. They are not out of place because inexplicable.

What is meant by such permissions we know not now, but we shall know hereafter; but meanwhile, we may understand enough to steady us when we see these things happening; and, perhaps, even to make us enter with some degree of fulness and power into the mind and will of God.

When money, and health, and influence, and the like, are taken away, there is in reality to them often the mystery of a higher call. So it was with Jesus. His sacred feet are seized, and nailed, and hindered, and man proclaims that they shall move no more.

But in that nailing they received the mystery of a higher call—they were given a wider sphere—the nail which pinned them to the cross enlarged the boundary of their mission, and gave them the world and not Judea for a sphere. He belonged to the Jews; but that nail lifted Him off the soil of the peculiar land; and not only were the Jews to look on Him whom they had pierced, but the nations also; and every one of us who feels that He was bruised for our iniquities—that by His stripes we are healed—and that it was our sins, as well as those of others, which nailed Him to the accursed tree.

And now with pierced feet Jesus traverses the *world*. Wherever the story of the cross reaches, so must it come as a tale of many woundings—

thus only can Jesus approach a poor sinner—yea, thus only wills He to approach him; and thus only should he, on his part, wish to see Him.

Who can tell what a prospect Jesus had from the cross? We are told that for the joy set before Him, He endured the cross, despising the shame—and this may have been one of the endurance helps. It was the will of His Father that Jesus should traverse Judea for awhile, bearing with Him blessing wherever He went; but that was to be only for a time—there was a deeper will to be fulfilled; and terrible as were the shame and pain of the cross, the words of Jesus' heart, as His feet were transfixed to it, were these, "I delight to do Thy will, O my God."

And, in truth, when we have served God with what we have had at our disposal, be it health, wealth, position, or anything else, and these are removed, by a providential dispensation, from us, we must not for a moment look upon ourselves as removed from the power to fulfil a high will of God, or a high destiny; we must rather seek to have our eyes open to see that we are now called to the fulfilment of a deeper will. And though we see it not, and flesh and blood would choose it not; our call has been to oneness in action with the mind of God, which mind has passed on into something deeper—more for the eternal glory, than anything that has hitherto been revealed as to our career.

The stillness of those feet of Jesus, nailed to the accursed tree, was a fulfilment of the deeper will of the Father. The hour had come—the time for it; and now activity must cease for a season, the sandal must be unbound, the nail must be infixed.

And may we see the fulfilment of 'will' in all our times of enforced cessation—it may be even painful cessation from service; in all our sad exchanges of that which is pleasant, for that which is hard to flesh and blood.

If we see that which is made ill use of taken away, we are inclined to say, 'it is a just judgment;' but if that which is being made a good use of, we are inclined to be staggered. But we shall not stagger, if we say to ourselves, 'I am now going into the deeper will—obedience is better than sacrifice; it is more to the glory of God that I should fulfil His will by apparent personal extinction, when He appoints that for me, than by any ministry, no matter how much in outward appearance, for His glory. "He must increase, but I must decrease," said the Baptist.

Let us steadily keep in view also the idea of *service*. When these feet of Jesus became pierced, they entered upon a higher form of service than they had yet assumed. The piercing was essential to this. The feet which had done well during life, were not now laid aside, they were placed in service of a different kind.

And as to us, let us never let go the idea of God's honouring us in service. If our will be like the will of Jesus, ready for aught that God wills, we shall never be thrown aside—we shall never be put down to lower service. We may be apparently so, but not really; for He who ordains our service knows what is in it—what of glory to Himself—what of honour to us.

Therefore, should all our instruments of usefulness fail us—even the very members of our body; let us but have faith and obedience, and let the mind which was in Jesus, as He allowed His feet to be nailed to the cross, be in us; and our apparent laying aside may be our highest service.

One more observation we would make. This piercing, which appeared to put an end to Jesus altogether, was, in point of fact, only an end to His human suffering. The long journeys were now all ended—the many wearinesses—the footsore of travel—the goings about far away from His Father's home.

The piercing of those feet was the way to everlasting rest—an unlikely way, to all human appearance; but the best way in the mind of God.

Ah! how little do we know of the way to long, deep rest! how different our way of seeking it from that in which it pleases God to send it! How often do we think our great trial can bring us no peace! while in very truth, in that may be wrapped up our great rest.

Sad indeed to every Christian must be the contemplation of the pierced feet of Jesus; but now as we look back upon the crucifixion, our feeling of sadness may be tempered with satisfaction. We think not only of what the piercings have done for *us*, but also of what they did for *Him*—that they ended a life of sorrow, and were the immediate preparations for the commencement of a life of unending and unutterable joy.

THE FEET WHICH HAD BEEN LOVINGLY TENDED.

There are no cups of such unmingled bitterness as not to have in them one drop of what is sweet; and the cup of life which Christ drank was no exception to the rule.

True! His smiles were few, His friends were few, sunshine did not often fall upon Him, but He did rejoice in spirit; there were some who loved Him —there were some homes where He was welcome— there were those who ministered to Him of their substance, who looked on Him with reverence, who outpoured to Him their hearts in love.

And so Jesus, fulfilling His lot as man, put Himself even by these small enjoyments under the terrible power of contrast.

These feet which are now pierced with the cruel nails, were once washed with tears, and wiped with the hair of a loving woman's head—they had been tended with unusual evidences of love.

It may have been that the remembrance of this love came along with the piercing of the nail; and that the mind of Jesus, acute in all its susceptibilities and powers, put the stroke of the executioner and the tenderness of the woman side by side.

It was but a little while before, and perhaps the contrast of the 'Hosannahs' and the 'Crucify Him' had given Him food enough for melancholy thought; and now the anointing with tears, and the transfixing with a nail, may have presented themselves side by side. In that intense rush of true human misery which, though He was the Son of God, yet came to Him on the cross as the Son of man, the weight of this contrast may have been felt.

It is a sad thought that, we cannot have any enjoyment but what carries within it a seed of possible sorrow. Pure and, so to speak, perfect as regards itself, as we look at it now, and turn it every way, we can see no trouble clinging to it, nor can we see why any should do so; but we are not able to look forward far enough, and to see how it will link itself with some future woe.

The laugh of the curly-headed child which now fills my heart with gladness, may be destined to make doubly bitter the hour when I shall be left alone; the whole oneness with a heart which beats with my heart may only make more lost, and bewildered, and lonely, my condition when that heart has ceased to beat. We do not say that such thoughts are to be indulged, or to be gone in search of; misery enough will come to meet us without going to look for it; we only say that in providing one of the two elements necessary for contrast, every present pleasure has in it the power of pointing with double anguish some future woe. "By the waters of Babylon we sat down and wept when we remembered thee, O Sion." "Oh that I were as in months past," says Job, "as in the days when God preserved me, when His candle shined upon my head, and when by His light I walked through darkness;" and then two whole chapters are filled with an account of what he had been, and what he then was. "When the builders laid the foundation of the temple of the Lord (Ezra iii) they set the priests in their apparel with trumpets, and the Levites, the sons of Asaph, with cymbals, to praise the Lord, after the ordinance of David, king of Israel. And they sang together by course in praising and giving thanks unto the Lord, because He is good, for His mercy endureth for ever toward Israel. And all the people shouted with a great shout, when they praised the Lord, because the foundation of the house was laid." But there were those who had seen another temple, and other days—they were old now, but their memory was young; and the power of contrast came with terrible force on them. "But many of the priests and Levites, and chief of the fathers, who were ancient men, that had seen the first house, when the foundation of this house was laid before their eyes, wept with a loud voice."

If Jesus had never experienced a kindness, never heard a Hosannah, never had a Mary to anoint Him, or a John to lie in His bosom, or even a grateful Gadarene to ask to be always with Him, His position on the cross would have been so far ameliorated that, it would have had less in it of this element of contrast.

But would it have been well that it should have been ameliorated—that even one drop of its bitterness should have been diluted, one grain of it removed? We may be sure it would not. Contrast works both ways, as from joy to sorrow, so from sorrow to joy. Our Lord notes the double action in John xvi: "Verily, verily, I say unto you, that ye shall weep and lament, but the world shall rejoice, and ye shall be sorrowful, but your sorrow shall be turned into joy;" then He illustrates it from a well-known fact in common life, and adds, "And ye now, therefore, have sorrow; but I will see you again, and your heart shall rejoice, and your joy no man taketh from you."

The power which wrought backward was able to work forward too; and as Jesus endured the cross, the joy set before Him no doubt wrought upon His mind.

It was with Jesus as we are sure it ever is with His people who suffer with a mind akin to His, the immense future was able to out-weigh altogether the little past; the joy that was gone was nothing, in comparison with that which was to come. He, as man, shared in the great law of bounty, by which His Father ordains that that which we sow, and allow to die at His command, shall spring up an hundred, and a thousand fold. The pierced One sowed a contrast to reap a contrast—the contrast of the preciousness of the little love He had experienced and His present piercing, with these same piercings and the future adorings of individuals, the love of millions—all those wonders of Revelation v—the falling down before the Lamb —the mingling of the voices of many angels round about the throne, and the living creatures, and the elders, whose number was ten thousand times ten thousand, and thousands of thousands; whose cry was this: 'Worthy is the Lamb that was slain to receive power, and riches, and wisdom, and strength, and honour, and glory, and blessing; the response to whose cry came loud and long from all places of which we have any ken; for every creature which is in heaven, and on the earth, and under the earth, and such as are in the sea, and all that are in them, re-echoed the ascription of praise; and said, Blessing and honour, and glory, and power, be unto

Him that sitteth upon the throne, and unto the Lamb for ever and ever; and the living creatures say amen, and the four-and-twenty elders fall down and worship Him that liveth for ever and ever.' As I write of this great glory, I can scarce believe that a moment ago I was at the cross; that it is at pierced feet the elders fall. I too say Amen. Thou hast right nobly won it all, O Christ. Amen and amen.

But now we must come back to ourselves, our little concerns; for in truth they are all-important to us, and our blessed Saviour knows that they are so. He will allow us to use His cross, on which He perfected our great atonement, as our teacher, our comforter in the contrasts, in the midst of which we are set. What a chapter might be written upon such deep condescensions of the cross —how it is our comforter as well as our reprover, our vivifier as well as our destroyer (of self); how it heals as well as wounds; how it whispers as well as thunders; how it stoops low beneath the humblest roofs, as well as towers high above the loftiest thrones.

The once lovingly tended, but now pierced feet of Jesus teach me, then, these lessons. When sorrow comes upon me I must meet the contrast of the present with the past, with another contrast—even that of the present with the future.

But to do this I must of course have a future.

I am privileged to sorrow, not as those without hope, but then I must have the hope.

And so it will be a good thing to dwell upon future blessedness, even when it is not wanted as a compensation for the present sorrow; to have the blessedness always vivid, always at hand. All thoughts of the future are not to be set down as dreamy and unpractical; our present is always connected with a past and a future; and we should let a blessed future exercise its power.

Alas! the world is full of those who have no future; those, whose chief thought concerning the future is to reduce it to nothingness as far as they can. The future can be no help to them. But it ought to be much to the believer; he should see it as God's antidote to sorrow. What it was to our Lord, it may well be to us.

We may be sure that our heavenly Father allows no trouble to come upon His people, without its own balancings and compensations. As no temptation is permitted without the means withal of escape, so no trouble without the means of endurance. But, as in the matter of the temptation, the way of escape is not always visible at once, so in that of trouble. We must recollect ourselves; we must call to mind the promised future; we must bring our spiritual being into the trial; and then will come the peace.

Another lesson which I learn is, 'the sobering power of contrast.'

Place of Personal Suffering. 189

These pierced feet are those which as we have seen were once anointed with very precious ointment; which were washed with tears; which were even wiped with the hairs of the head. When we remember that thus it was with the Lord, how will it balance us when we seem likely to be intoxicated by present honour, or respect, or wealth, or joy! To be taken by force one day, to be made a king, and ere long to be taken by force to a cross, has its counterpart oftentimes in our life.

Who is there that has not suffered from unbalanced joy; that has not at some time been run away with by the steed on whose neck he flung the rein; that has not been content with what 'is,' careless about what 'may be'! We have probably all suffered more or less from not having kept ourselves in hand; but we probably have experiences enough to fall back upon, if we will only call them to mind, from which we can choose correctives for the future, able to balance us by the power of contrast.

Another voice which comes to me from this cross, to which are affixed the pierced feet, is this. Let us do what in us lies to tend while we can; the time may come when we cannot, but must stand helplessly by. Our Lord Himself says, "the poor ye have always with you, but me ye have not always."

No ointment could be poured on the feet when on the cross—the time had passed for that; they who would have anointed those feet with their life-blood if they could, can now do no more than stand helplessly by.

Even as regards earthly love and its tender ministrations, the cross condescends to teach this lesson. It says, 'Shew love while thou canst. What thou hast opportunities in abundance to do to-day, thou mayest soon be debarred from doing for ever. Even in such little things as these, what bitter thoughts may we lay up for ourselves, e.g, slowly and painfully we see some dear one drag one leg after the other; a long day's journey now, from the bed to the sofa, and from the sofa to the bed again; how glad we should now be to walk miles with him; but we recall the time when we refused to go here or there at his request to gratify him. With eyes half closed some dear one lies the live long day, and when they are opened it is weariedly and languidly, to be closed again without having taken any notice; and we sit by the bedside and think, how we refused, at some time or other, to shew him something, or to gladden that eye with a cheerful look or smile. Perhaps, even in the matter of the day's food we cared but little to make it palatable; and now we lay dainties beside the sick one's couch, but it is too late, they are untasted—even untouched; the time for being able to minister has past. Its season was in daily life; but they knew not the time, and now it has slipped away beyond their reach.

Place of Personal Suffering.

The cross, in its graciousness of teaching, condescends even to these things, and says, 'In common life-love let it not be so.' I would echo the voice of the cross. I would say, 'Lay up for yourself, so far as it may be done in and by things of this life, strong consolations by a life-long ministry of love. Be sowing seed every day you live, which shall sprout, and ear, and be garnered by the bed side, by the coffin and grave side of those you love. Those who sow facts shall reap memories; and memories shall do wonders when the time comes for them to act. They will sit by the lonely hearth and people it; they will come into the desolate heart and sing in it; they will command the desert to blossom as the rose, and turn the dry ground into water springs. Fresh herbage carpets the road side of the one who has yet many milestones to pass alone; and however dusty and hard his daily walk, he may turn aside and journey onwards amid the freshness of the dew of herbs; every loving word and deed in the past is like a grass blade—each one distinct—all offering themselves as a velvet pile to his tender feet. If to dwell in unity be like the dew of heaven —like what dew, in its sparkling and refreshing, must it be to have dwelt amid perfect and unwearied ministries of love!'

But enough of ourselves, we must turn back again to Christ; the voice of teaching says, 'tend thou His pierced feet while thou canst.'

But how can we, for now His feet are like unto fine brass, as though it burned in a furnace.

He Himself has told us how it may be done. "Inasmuch as ye have done it unto one of the least of these, my brethren, ye have done it unto me."

Let us picture to ourselves what our feelings would be, if we were now to see the feet of Jesus nailed to the cross. As we stood by them and looked up into that pain-stricken yet patient face, we should say, 'What can I do for the One hanging there for me?' we should say, 'What could I ever have done which I have left undone?' We should question ourselves, and no doubt condemn ourselves too.

But we are more favourably circumstanced than this. No doubt we have much to condemn ourselves for, for we have left undone that which we should have done, but as yet there is time to do. Yes, we may, as it were, give comfort to the One upon the cross; we may spend upon Him, we may tend Him. Let us do so while we can. The day will certainly come when we can do so no more, not because Jesus' feet are wounded afresh, but because we shall have passed out of the sphere in which it is appointed that such things may be done. We believe that there will be plenty of glorious service in the life to come; but we believe that all such as is connected with fellowship in Christ's sufferings must cease.

Much of present service is of this character; if we would perform such ministrations of love we must do so now.

No doubt, the so doing will bring its own peculiar reward. That reward will probably connect itself with the sweetness of memory's retrospects. We need no vivid imagination to picture it to ourselves. Just think for a moment of looking at those feet in glory with the marks, the ineffable marks of the nails in them; and of being able to hold sweet talk within ourselves about what we did for them, and to them. The time will have passed for all such sayings as, 'When saw we Thee an hungered, and fed Thee; sick or in prison, and visited Thee.' We shall know all about that; it will be explained to us how it was, and we [knowing then the connection between Jesus and His people] shall understand it. And we shall feel, 'O how sweet to think that I did not neglect those precious feet; that I eased them, that I honoured them, that I anointed, washed, wiped them; that once I rested them, and ever, dust-covered as they were, honoured them.' Would it not be heaven just to go about saying that to ourselves? and oh, how much more a heaven to hear Jesus saying it to us; and, perhaps, to meet with others, now this one and now that, and to hear from them what they did, and to tell them what we did. 'Stay,' perhaps the reader says, this will foster pride; 'did not the accepted ones say, shamefacedly, that they had done nothing at all?' Ah, yes, but as we have said, the time for this has past; they believe what Jesus spake, when He said how they had done it to His very self; they have no false modesty any more than foolish pride; all things are now seen in their real light, and they shall know the full value of what they did, and rejoice in it, and perhaps hold sweet communion with each other about it.

With the close of this life, and our passage from this scene of sorrow, ends the opportunity for all this; let us lay up, then, for ourselves this treasure in heaven—sweet memories, ever to be renewed at the sight of the One who was pierced for us.

There is one more remark to be made ere we pass on from this branch of the subject. We must expect vicissitudes even as they were the portion of our Lord.

We would fain always have the tendings and the tenderness of love—an even life; but as He was upon the earth, even so are we. Therefore, when the changes come, let us betake ourselves to the cross. Let us sit down, not at the feet of some Gamaliel to teach us philosophy, but at the pierced feet of Jesus, to learn the philosophy of the cross. To us it may now be a still, calm place; we may just sit there and think—look and think, and think and look again. I say nothing of the thorns in the head, or the nails in the hands, or the wound in the side; I see enough in this my time of woful change, to calm, and teach, and strengthen my heart, if I use the sight aright, in the once lovingly tended, but now pierced, 'feet of Jesus.'

CHAPTER XII.

THE ANGELS SITTING AT THE HEAD AND FEET OF THE PLACE WHERE THE BODY OF JESUS HAD LAIN.

"And as she wept, she stooped down, and looked into the sepulchre, and seeth two angels in white sitting, the one at the head, and the other at the feet, where the body of Jesus had lain:" JOHN XX, 12.

THE birth of Jesus was heralded by an angel, and the choirs of the heavenly host sang in chorus words, the depth of which we cannot fathom, simple though they seem, "Glory to God in the highest, and on earth, peace, good will towards men."

And at His death the angels were present too. Had Jesus but prayed to His Father, presently twelve legions of the soldiers of the skies would have appeared. He prayed not for the legions, for all that fierce strife which was to be undergone in the work of our salvation, He was to be engaged in alone; yet even in this an angel was seen strengthening Him.

We know not how many of them were about the cross, when He drooped His head, and said, "'It is finished,' and gave up the ghost;" but we can well believe that they were there.

And now that all is over, we find them at the grave, and in it—an angel rolling away the great stone and sitting on it; and two sitting within the sepulchre, the one at the head, and the other at the feet, where the body of Jesus had lain.

They were certainly present at the ascension; for when the cloud received Him out of His disciples' sight; and while they looked steadfastly towards heaven as He went up, behold two men stood by them in white apparel, which also said, "Ye men of Galilee, why stand ye gazing up into heaven, this same Jesus which is taken up from you into heaven, shall so come in like manner, as ye have seen Him go into heaven;" (Acts i, 11,) and when the Son of Man comes again, it shall be in His own glory, and in His Father's, and in that of the holy angels. (Luke ix, 26.)

It is given to us to know but little of the ministry and nature of angels; and there would be little practical use in our speculating thereon. We do not propose to ourselves any such speculative inquiry now; but rather the gathering up of such thoughts as present themselves to us of a practical nature, and calculated to be of help and blessing to us in our own spiritual life.

If we were asked to state specifically the one

object for which those angels were sitting at the head and foot of that empty space, so lately occupied by the body of the Lord, we should decline attempting any answer. For we feel that we are here in the presence of much mystery.

But though we cannot see the actual source from which the light comes, we are able to see some glimmerings of great use to us; and we would thankfully gather them into as close a focus as we can.

Had it been written that the body was there, and that the angels were seen sitting or standing at its actual head and feet, we could have understood many reasons for this; but now the body is gone, and as to this empty space, what do these angelic beings, waiting there?

As we have said, we will gather up such thoughts as it has pleased God to give us on this matter.

They need not be ranged strictly in order, for the object is practical teaching for our own souls.

The dead body of our Lord is in itself now certainly helpless. It had been willingly helpless when nailed to the cross; it was now forsaken for a season of the living principle, and was dead, just as our bodies are when they feel no touch, when they cannot move.

We know that even after the spirit has departed from it, great importance may be attached to the mere body itself. Satan was most anxious to get possession of the body of Moses, and Michael the archangel contended with him about it. And if the evil one was desirous of getting possession of the one body, we can well understand how much more anxious would he be to get possession of the other. He doubtless knew enough of the importance of that body to make him wish to have it in his keeping, or to deal with it, as he saw fit, however that may be.

That body was of supreme importance in many ways which even we can see.

It was wanted for presentation in glory, as the accepted ransom—and for the visible headship of redeemed humanity—and for the witness of the carrying out of the plans of the Father—and for governmental purposes hereafter—and for the adoration, and deep affection of the saints; yes, and as the object of the Father's love, for "the Father loveth the Son," the whole Son, as God and man.

These reasons, and many others which will readily suggest themselves to the reader's mind we can see; others, and it may be far deeper ones, there are which we cannot see.

And Satan we may be sure was abroad at this time, and looking with no indifferent eye upon the body of the Lord.

We know not what evil spirits may have attempted against it, had they not been guarded against; and these may have been the two angels who, set at the head and feet, had been appointed to hold watch and ward over that which when deserted of its spirit, was as helpless as any of the dead. Or, perhaps, they were but two of a goodly host, which had been engaged in that especial work.

Now, all the helplessness of the dead body of the Lord is very comforting to us—that wrapping in the linen cloth—that laying in the tomb—and notably, the guardianship of these angels at the head and feet.

In the times when we have to do with death, we need every possible comfort. And when we are busy with our dead, showing all that last sad care which they can receive from us; when the helplessness of that which was once perhaps so helpful to us forms one of the terrible elements of our distress; then let us bear in mind the helplessness of the body of the One, who was even the Lord of life. Let us say, 'so handled they the body of my Lord; so was it, even as this.'

Who can tell what strength such a thought will give us, how we shall pass away from our lower death to that higher death; how, wondering that Jesus should ever undergo the like of what we see before us, we shall be comforted and say, 'It is with my dear one, dead in Christ, only as it was with the Lord when dead Himself.'

There is power in bringing the incidents of the helplessness of Christ into the incidents of the helplessness with which we have now to do; and not only power, but peace. But there are two lessons which it will be especially well to learn here. One is, that a necessary part of the machinery of God's great plan (or even ours) may be apparently helpless, while in reality it is guarded, (for after vivification.)

When Jesus' body lay helplessly in the grave, to all human appearance, heaven had ended with it. No human being could possibly, unless so far as he had apprehended the doctrine of the resurrection, have divined that anything more could be expected from it. The disciples knew not that He should rise from the dead; (John xx, 9,) and if they did not, we may be sure that no one else did either. There was no higher thought in the mind of any than to embalm it, and finally entomb it, to weep over it, to enshrine it in memory; but never, so far at least as this world was concerned, to associate it with life again.

But living angels were watching that helpless body; the life of the other world gathered around the death of this. And even when the body had gone, they stayed; it may be that it was necessary for provision to be made even that those grave clothes, and that napkin should not be disturbed; that all should be orderly and calm; that it should be seen that heaven was there. True the disciples did not see this latter, that was reserved for Mary; but she did, and passed on the truth to us.

How often we are confounded by the thought that what appeared to be an essential part of the machinery of God's plan has broken down. It may be something in the church, something in our families and homes, or in our own souls; this breach has fallen not upon some accessory or incidental, but upon something essential; and all seems reduced to helplessness.

But if this thing be of God, apparent is not real ruin. All is guarded; life is about all, the higher life of heaven, powers of another world.

Even when the body of Jesus had gone, and the place where it had lain was empty, there were witnesses from above for her to whom the revelation was to come that, the interests of heaven were still there; and that all was not ended about that body, because it was not at that moment lying there.

To her, the weakest, was the revelation made; to her, who would not go from the spot; who was chained to it by the exigency and attraction of tenderest love.

Let us learn what this can teach us. We have the advantage of looking back to the plan of God, and understanding it as a whole. And this is our lesson here; when we know that God is in a matter, and failure seems to come into that matter, let us believe that God will be true to His own great plan, and that all is watched over, all provided for, for a fresh incoming of life. Many plans cannot come out into full glory of life without an intervening period of death; but all death, which is part of the plan, is meant to come forth into resurrection life. Therefore, during the death period, let us see the heavenly guardings, angels at the head and feet of where, what we had expected so much from, had lain.

The next lesson which suggests itself to us, is this. As there are agents of attack invisible, (and often to us perplexing,) so are there angels and means of defence invisible also.

And, in truth, we are in a world full of perplexities in this way. We feel ourselves from time to time suddenly struck at from one side and another. We are struck down, from quarters whence we never could have expected it; we are struck fiercely, even as our Lord, whose body was brought to that tomb by a traitor's kiss. The eater of our bread becomes the lifter up of the heel against us. Now there is nothing more terrifying than the unseen; to feel that we may at any moment be under its influence, and that we have no means of defending ourselves against it.

Our comfort lies here, that we have friends as well as foes in the unseen. The angels of God are ascending and descending, while we lie with our head pillowed upon a stone; the mountain compassed with horses and chariots of man, is full of horses and chariots of fire, (2 Kings vi, 17.) Man as in this case may be the agent, or he may not be; the teaching is that, 'whatever the attack, by whom, or from whence, God has the means to meet it.'

And so, when we think of the invisible world with all its awe and wonders, with all its bearings upon ourselves, and tremble at the mystery with which we are surrounded, especially when we come to think of death and the grave, and the spirit world, let us think of the friends whom we have there. They could be made visible to us in a moment; they will be at the right time. When the right time came, they were seen by Mary, so will they be by us.

In the following incidents, the reader will see how, when we think all is helpless, or hopeless, or forgotten, God has His own agencies at work. That which we think to be forgotten, is remembered before Him with power.

"Let us take courage!" said Luther to Melancthon, after a day of despondency, when their enemies were strongest, and Heaven's help seemed to be withdrawn. Through a thin partition, they had just heard their children's voices rising up in trustful prayer to God for the victory of His truth, and the strengthening of their fathers for the fight. "Let us take courage—the giants are praying for us."

In a volume recently published, called "The Man with the Book, or the Bible among the People," the writer, an agent of the London City Mission, gives an account of his first entrance on Mission work in a most unpromising sphere—Paradise Court. The missionary was a young man, and the field of labour wholly unturned by the gospel plough, or unsown with gospel seed, was full of rankest weeds—nothing but misery, ribaldry, profanity, poverty, and disease met the young man during his visitation all the day.

His own words will best convey his heart's despondency. One

But the great thing is to believe that the invisible is instinct with holy influences for us, with living friends for us; that in its darkness there are beings clothed in light to whom God has given charge as concerning us.

scene of misery, temporal and spiritual, after another he describes, and then he says, "After failing to convey religious instruction to the people at the next house, the young missionary left the place in a state of mind exactly opposite to that in which he had entered it in the morning. A sense of inefficiency, of utter disqualification for the work had taken possession of his mind, and damped his zeal. To have instructed the respectable poor, to have removed the difficulties of men in error would have been a pleasure, but to evangelize such a people as the dwellers in Paradise Court and its surroundings seemed hopeless. Besides the offensiveness of the work, the thought of spending six or more hours daily in those wretched dwellings, subjected to the risk of contagion, insult, and personal violence, and that, with such feeble hope of benefitting the people, produced a sense of regret that the effort had been made. So powerfully did these reasons act, that the missionary availed himself of the consideration that Saturday would be an inconvenient day for the people, and stayed away; but on Sunday afternoon, about three o'clock, he approached the Court with a faint heart, and a bundle of tracts in his hand."

Then comes an account of fresh insults and threats; and now God shewed him that he was not alone in that place, that all was not dark, that there were some there, though hitherto he had seen them not, who were arrayed in light.

The missionary was giving tracts away, and speaking some friendly words to the people standing at their doors, when his work was stayed by unexpected sounds which proceeded from an upper room.

They fell so strangely on the ear, that he stood still and gazed up at the windows, with the exclamation upon his lips, "Surely the Lord has His hidden ones in this place."

An effort was evidently being made in one of the rooms to sing

The invisible in its bright as well as in its dark side is in connection with me; why should I take to myself all the gloom, and leave all the light. There is a mystery of evil under which I suffer; there is a mystery of love in which is healing and a song of praise. A cracked female voice was trying to lead other voices, not one of which had been attuned to melody, in singing the hymn:

> "Come ye that love the Lord,
> And let your joys be known."

A woman at one of the windows, seeing the astonishment of the visitor, said, "It's Widow Peters, Master, having a meeting; she lives here, in the first back. She's a good un, the dear old soul is like a mother to us." The visitor approached the room, and, as the singing ceased, opened the door. He saw at a glance that the company consisted of five very poor women. Four were seated on the frame of the bedstead, and another at the table, upon which lay an open Bible and hymn-book. "This is he," exclaimed one of the women, "This is the Tract-man who is coming to read to us out of the blessed book." Upon this the widow rose, her countenance beaming with holy joy, and with that graceful dignity which a religious life often confers upon the poor, offered her hand to the missionary, exclaiming, "Come in, sir, come in, and let us praise the Lord together. I have pleaded with Him for poor souls in this place, and now He has sent His messenger with glad tidings; may the Lord bless you to many." This welcome was given with such genuine feeling, that the messenger was overpowered. The speaker was aged. Quite seventy years had whitened her few remaining hairs, and given a decrepit appearance to her slender frame, but under the influence of strong religious feeling she stood erect, and the feebleness of her voice gave peculiar force to words which entered the soul. The poor women felt it as they stood with tearful eyes, and the young missionary felt it, for the only answer was an affectionate holding of that withered hand in his, and a reverential gazing into the face of the old disciple.

help. If the first must be mine, the second may. The tomb and the angels go together; two angels in white, sitting, the one at the head, and the other at the feet, where the body of Jesus had lain.

But we must not turn from this part of our subject without noting the witness which was here given to the one who loved the Lord, that, although certainly helpless, still the body had been cared for by heaven itself.

I can quite understand how it was to a woman, that in this aspect, this manifestation was made.

From Mary's address to the one whom she thought to be the gardener, we know how great was her distress at the body having been removed; let her but know where it was, and she would take it away. All she thought about it was, that in its helplessness it had been carried off, and whither, and by whom, and why?

Before the young missionary left the room, the aged woman prayed for him, and what he says of himself is this: "That prayer was blessed to the young missionary. As he stepped into the Court, he felt that the coward spirit had left him, and that he had received power to intercede with the Almighty for perishing souls. His heart was too full to speak to the people; but as he passed their doors, a cry of holy desire for their salvation (that best preparation for the work of an evangelist) ascended to where Jesus, the Mediator, is seated at the right hand of God."

We may rest assured that it is thus far oftener than we suppose. God's lights are burning even in our darkest scenes of trial, our most discouraging spheres of duty, if only we have eyes to see them; and so go on our way in peace.

For one with such feelings heaven had a voice, as it ever will have; and surely the sight of these angels—God's own ministers, sitting at the head and feet of the place where the body of Jesus had lain, was enough to tell her that, that which she loved had been well cared for, cared for by One far stronger than any human friend—by God Himself. God has many witnessing voices for those who are in distress by reason of love. When we are in sorrow, that His interests seem dead and even taken out of sight, or from any cause of love; because we, like the bride in Canticles, cannot find the one whom our soul loveth, God will not leave us helplessly and hopelessly ever to gaze into the darkness and emptiness of a tomb; beings of light shall head and foot our sorrow, and their voices shall ask 'Why weepest thou?'

Though Mary, in the intensity of her grief, and by reason of the quick appearance of the Lord Himself, had not time to say more, or hear more; and may have failed to gather up all these thoughts; still we, for whose learning these things are written, looking back calmly upon the whole transaction, may accept them; and with no light better than twilight around us, and nothing but grave darkness before us, be encouraged by the assurance that in connection with our woes, are angels clothed in white.

One word more, ere we part with the helpless body of the Lord. Mary's whole thought seemed to be as though she, and those who were associated with her, were the only ones who could do anything for it; but God taught her His higher care for it. And as to us, we think of all our care of the dear body while we had it (and sometimes, perhaps, we, in the excess of love, write bitter things morbidly against ourselves, as though we might have done more), and we so think as though we only could care for it, or would do so better than God, or as though He would neglect it.

He neglected not the body which Mary so well loved, He did better by it than she could have done; she could only have bought spices wherewith to embalm it, He sent even angels to watch over it.

Let us think of our dear departed ones as being encompassed with a love superior to ours, as having invisible guardians taking care of all concerning them—the head and feet. Let us think indeed of our love, let us dwell upon it, let our memories be charged with the devotion which we bear to our dead; but ever let it be to connect it with the thought that, there is One who loves them better than we could do; and whose sweet ministry of love, though invisible, is sure; as was that sitting of the angels, though for awhile unseen, at the head and feet of the place where the body of Jesus had lain.

Honour from Heaven for the Whole Rejected One.

This is another thought which strikes our mind in connection with the two angels—one at the head and another at the feet of the place where the body of Jesus had lain.

It is one which will commend itself with both sweetness and power, to such as love Christ and wish Him to be their All in all, as regards both this life and that which is to come.

The angels were at the place of the thorn-crowned head, and at that of the pierced feet. That tomb occupied a double position. It was the place of rejection by the world. Man's worst efforts against his enemy is to get him into the grave; therefore Jesus lying in the grave was in the place of rejection by the world.

But it was something more—it was double sided. It was at once in deep shadow, and in bright sunshine. If it was a place of rejection by the world, it was one of reception by His own. God had provided a tomb offered by love, for the body cast out by hate.

It was something more also. That tomb was a place of reception by His Father. The angels are a witness to this. In all probability, angel watchers had charge over that body from the moment when the bitter cry "It is finished" went forth, and the

Lord gave up the ghost. At any rate, we know they are in the tomb; and angels all clothed in white are not to be found in the mansions of the dead, except on high commission from God.

That tomb, with the angels in it, binds together, for all God's people who suffer for Him, the two ideas of rejection and reception. Let us so bind them in our minds. We are often greatly depressed by rejection, especially when it is carried to the last extent; but it does not go as far with us as it did with Jesus; and where it is deepest, there reception is largest—the tomb and the angels are together.

If we be wise, we shall look for our comfort not so much to any alleviations of man's hate, as to manifestations of God's love. Of these last we may be sure. They will be always special, always proportioned to the need—an angel to strengthen in the time of weakness, angels of light in the tomb of darkness, witnesses from heaven of acceptance, when the evidence of rejection is strongest from the world.

A thought of the fulness of Christ's work comes also into the mind. Christ's was pre-eminently a full work, so to speak from head to feet—there were many piercings of thorns in the one, there were the piercings of the nails in the others. Corresponding to the two are the evidences of heavenly appreciation, honour, and love—an angel sitting at the head and another at the feet. The head—the seat of thought, and the feet—the instruments of motion—in both of which He had honoured His Father, and wrought a full work for us, are angel-guarded and God-honoured in death. And these embrace all—as we should say 'all from head to foot'; the hands and the heart also pierced, which lay between.

Now this thought also should be precious to us. There is a witness of fullness in the tomb. All we can hope for is through the death of Jesus; therefore that fulness is of the utmost importance to us. We say 'All of Him for all of us'—His head for mine, His heart for mine, His hands for mine, His feet for mine. I am unholy in all, He is holy in all; I am condemned in all, He is accepted in all; Heaven's witness to Him, if I am one with Him, becomes Heaven's witness also to me; I am cleansed from the impurity of thought and act, and am received in Him.

Let us not lightly part with this blessed thought of completeness in all its forms—the completeness of rejection meeting with that of reception, the thoroughly outcast for us, thoroughly God-honoured and received for us also.

For Completeness is an all-important idea; it is one of great working power in our daily life.

It gives clearness, and simplicity, and strength. It presents one great thought to the mind, and only one, because that one is all-sufficient. There is always great power in concentration; and the simple believer has this advantage, he lives with an abiding concentrated thought. We have not to be ever thinking what we can do for ourselves, but what He has done for us; our minds need not dissipate their strength in wandering over a number of subjects, they may abide here; and when we go forth to act, it will be in power derived hence.

Here, and here only, lies our joy. We can have little joy in ourselves; our attainments, even at the best, are so imperfect, the sense of incompleteness in character and all else is so depressing that, unless we have some point of perfection on which to dwell and rest, we shall find no peace, much less joy. But there is both joy and peace in believing (Rom. xv, 13). The perfect Christ is all sufficient for imperfect man; the mind gathers its thoughts in on Him, the heart its affections; they cannot go beyond perfection, and perfection they have found in Him.

Just in proportion as we fail to see the wholeness of Jesus for our need of acceptance and righteousness, shall we feel discomfort and weakness. The way to look at him is as entirely crucified, Head and feet, and entirely honoured, Head and feet too —"two angels sitting, the one at the head, and the other at the feet, where the body of Jesus had lain."

THE PRESENCE OF THE ANGELS AT THE FIRST AND AT THE SECOND BIRTH OF CHRIST.

At the commencement of this chapter we noted the presence of the angels at the birth of Christ—how all heaven was moved at it, and witnessed it. In all the words and anthems and appearance of the angels on that occasion, there was heaven's conferring of dignity upon a helpless period. There is but little dignity connected with infancy, especially in its earliest days; but this child, though in all human points to be as other children, yet was in heaven's witnessings to be above them all.

This period, helpless though it was, had one aspect which made it well worthy of the dignity conferred upon it. It was the beginning of *life*—life with all its possibilities; and those possibilities in His case so assured in the purposes of God, as to be practically realities.

The Father only knew the possibilities which lay before the life, or rather wrapped up in the life of the infant of Bethlehem—possibilities reaching out into eternity, having to do with what is doubtless the grandest outputting of the divine mind, viz., the salvation of man; and the attendance and psalmody of angels, of the great multitude of the heavenly host was very fit to accompany this great event.

What marvel was it that at such a birth, the multitudes of the heavenly host should have praised God! It may be that there were many things which they desired to look into in the matter, but they knew enough to bind heaven and earth together in that burst of praise and blessing.

So here, upon the helpless period which we have already been considering. The grave was the place of helplessness, but it was also the cradle of the resurrection. Just as the place where Jesus lay at His first entrance into life contained all the possibilities of the Saviour's after great career, so the place where He lay when He had for a short season departed out of life, contained the possibilities of that great career which beginning at the resurrection from the dead, was to go on into eternity itself.

The grave answered all its purpose, in being a thorough witness to Christ's death, and a temporary resting place for His dead body; but its office was to be but very temporary indeed, so far as the past was concerned. It had its future also; it protected and sheltered for the short season during which this was required, a body with a great future life. And now, natural life is ended, the feeble breath which had been drawn stronger and stronger into manhood, had just been expired upon the cross; the great possibilities of that child had been wrought out into realities in life and death, and a second period of helplessness had come—it was the preliminary to the second—the resurrection life; Jesus had one birth in an inn, he was to have another in a grave.

Before *this* helpless body also, there lie great possibilities. Let it but be quickened into life, and follow out its vast destinies, and the victory over the grave would be secure—the kingdom of heaven would be opened, the race of man would be delivered, and all the wide scheme of redemption would be fulfilled.

Viewing the sepulchre in this light, we can easily understand how the angels of God had some business there.

Our views of the grave ought to be moulded on these views of the grave of Jesus. We are too much accustomed to look at the tomb with the idea of finality—associating it only with thoughts of life ended, helplessness completed, whereas we should think of it with ideas of life to come. We should associate it with great possibilities, we should think of its helplessness as only temporary. The cross of Christ is ours, with its peculiar teachings and power, so should also His grave be. As with Him we have died, so with Him in one sense we have arisen, in yet another we shall; and what His grave was to Him, that should ours be to us—the place of great possibilities; and those possibilities secured by the faithfulness of a covenant God.

Jesus might have been said to have been a

homeless One at His first birth. There was no room for Him in the inn. But the angels of God gave that homeless One a testimony which marked Him above all the sons of kings, cradled in the richest luxury that the world could afford.

And Jesus was in a homeless place at His second birth. He was in no grave of His own. He was not laid with His fathers after the flesh; but in His stranger grave tarried angels of God, as though to say how heaven can make up for aught which we may want, of all which should have been ours, according to the right and custom, or even the sentiment of earth.

The angels of God are, I doubt not, with us; and a father's honour, and a father's care in our most helpless and homeless seasons.

These two were eminently combined in Jacob when he laid his head upon the stone; and never was there a plainer manifestation of angels than to him as he slumbered there.

Let us remember that, what may be homeless as regards earth, may be richly furnished as regards heaven; what is dark and lonely here, may be light and peopled thence. This thought of the angels is very helpful in dispelling the ideas of the loneliness of the grave.

There was homelessness, yet heaven, at the two extreme points of Jesus' life—His birth—His death—a voice to us showing how the two may co-exist. None so loved of God as He; yet, when

He came forth in ministry for His Father, none without a place wherein to lay his head save He.

That grave we may remark in passing was but a lodging, it was not 'home;' and never should the grave be spoken of, or thought of, as any more than this by the people of God. A lodging for a little while was all that Joseph of Arimathea could offer at the best, and that is all that even the most honoured grave can give us.

It was amid friends that Jesus rose—the angels of God; and when the time comes for His people to rise, they shall do the like. The angels who were busy at the resurrection of the Lord, will not be wanting at the resurrection of His people also. Let the resurrection time have no terrors for us; such as be Christ's shall find in that day the angels to be with them, even as they were with their Lord.

THE ADDRESS OF THE ANGELS AT THE HEAD AND FEET WHERE THE BODY OF JESUS HAD LAIN.

The heart of man has often left the gay and lightsome dwellings of the living, and chosen its home in the sepulchre of the dead. Where the treasure is, there will the heart be also; and

Christ was Mary's treasure, therefore His sepulchre was her heart's home.

Christ was her treasure—Christ whether alive or dead; and as she had loved to be near Him in life, so also she would keep close to Him in death; for her affections were like the tendrils of the ivy which will twine around the root, and embrace the shattered trunk long after the glory of the tree has passed away, after it has ceased to be praised for the richness of its fruit, or to be sought for the refreshment of its shade.

No spot on earth was there which possessed her affections so much as that which held the body of her Lord; at His sepulchre she therefore now is found. And had He remained there like the ordinary dead, so long as Mary lived, she would in all probability day by day have been a pilgrim to His tomb.

And if we can imagine how Mary clung to the sepulchre so long as she knew only of a dead Christ, can we not imagine how her heart afterward soared upward when she thought of an ascended Christ.

Uninstructed love will ever tarry around the tomb of the saints, enlightened love will soar upward to their heavenly home.

When once Mary knew that her Lord had indeed ascended up on high, we can well imagine that she followed Him with her heart's adoring love; and that she contemplated Him no longer laid out in the darkness of death in His tomb, but seated in the magnificence of royalty upon His throne.

Now, however, she was in sorrow; and her sorrow, as is so often the case with the afflictions of God's people, is full of teaching for His church.

Before we speak of the address of the angels at the head and feet, let us note for a moment the tenacity of Mary's love. It is embodied in the narrative. When even he who was famous amongst the apostles for his loving heart had gone away unto his own house, this weak woman still clung around the spot which had so lately held the dead. Weeping but not complaining, standing without in what was to others the light of day, yet looking within in all steadfastness upon what was to her the mournful darkness of the tomb, the Magdalene is the picture of many a patient Christian in the gloom and perplexity of sorrow, whose tears are unseen but by the Lord, and whose earnest gaze is rewarded by a vision of light within the grave.

Thus standing, thus stooping, thus looking, the solitary mourner may be a great preacher to each of us. She is an incarnation of a noble truth—of the tenacity of true love. She minds us of how we should cling to Christ; how there is a special blessing in every demonstration of affection towards Him. She who stood, and wept, and looked, had more bestowed upon her than was vouchsafed to those who entered the sepulchre, and then returned to their own home.

May we be possessed of such a love, as under the most perplexing of circumstances will keep us clinging fast to Christ. It is a great thing to hold fast by faith, it is still greater to hold fast by love. Faith will make us step forward with courage into the dark, love will make even the darkest of God's dispensations light. Mary wept, because in her slowness of comprehension she, like others, had not apprehended the resurrection from the dead; but Mary soon rejoiced; the measure of her ignorance was counted as nothing, when compared with her immeasurable love.

As to us, whatever may be our spiritual perplexities, may our love hold fast to Christ. Ours may be a weeping love, for we are only in the flesh; but let it be also a tenacious love, for this will characterize it as from the heart. In all perplexities, when we cannot account for anything which has taken place; in all privations, when we feel as though the evening had removed our Saviour from our sight; in all isolations, when like Mary we seem to be left utterly alone, when our fellow disciples have gone each one to his own home, let us love the apparently absent Christ, even as we loved the present One. And who can tell whether it will not be with us, even as it was with the mourner to whom the angels, and then the Lord Himself appeared; whether He whom we thought was taken away will not prove very near; whether love which bridges over all chasms, annihilates all distances, and spans with one glowing arch the space between heaven and earth, will not enable us quickly to see and hear our Lord, and to fall before His feet, now more glorious than ever He had appeared before.

To this woman full of sorrow and love the angels manifest themselves—to her they speak. And even the bare fact of their addressing her at all is not without some teaching for us.

We might have held them excused from noting and sympathising with her sorrow by reason of the loftiness of their nature, and also of the functions which they were performing. Whatever those functions were, we may be sure they were of high import, for they were appointed to them by God. Had they been mere human watchers, though invisible, and been acting after the general manner of men, they would in all probability have let Mary come and go without showing themselves, or addressing her at all.

Though there were (as there still doubtless are) many things which the angels desired to look into in connection with the wonders of the cross, still they had knowledge enough to know that there was high connection between Jesus the crucified and recently buried One, and such as this weeping woman, stooping and looking in, and crying bitterly the while.

They were assisting at mysteries, and performing the part assigned therein to them; but sitting at the head and feet where the marks of human suffering had so lately been, they had an affinity for woe—woe connected with those very hands and feet—they were to minister to one who wept for the weeper, for the man of sorrows and acquainted with grief.

No doubt the relationship between a soul and Christ in all its fulness—the relation of the whole church—the union surpassing anything which the heavenly host can ever attain, is full of mystery to them; but they know enough about it to make them full of interest and sympathy, and of willingness to stoop low, yes, to any depth, to minister to those who are the heirs of salvation. They see them in their connection with the One who is the Lord of angels as well as men; and are ready with sympathy and honour to perform for them whatever service they are commanded by God.

A practical lesson surely for ourselves. How apt is high position to take away sympathies with the lowly—how often when we are set manifestly to the performance of some high function, do we allow the function to uplift ourselves—yes, and how often, under the pretence of being altogether taken up with some mission, or some spiritual effort or occupation, do we keep ourselves apart from those in sorrow, and remain silent, without a question as to why they weep.

In truth no functions, no positions, bid us not to give ourselves to tearful ones who are in sympathy with Christ; these retain their dignity, their place, even as they did for the angels; but they who are set in them should be ready with the " Why weepest thou?"

And now observe the method of their address. They say to her, 'Woman.' (*Gr.* γυνη.) It was a title of respect, such an one as we should use, when we said Mistress or Madam, or something similar thereto. It was not Woman, as an earthly being, and so as distinct from themselves—the angels of God—but 'Woman,' as one to be addressed with honour.

The use of this title of courtesy and respect by such beings and in such a place, opens out to us the beautiful thought of the condescension and courtesy of heavenly beings.

The thought is not without its comfort and its teaching too, in this rude pushing world, where the weak ones are thrust to the wall; and where one's nerves are grated and jarred continually with rough sights and words, and discourtesies of many a kind.

Courtesy is a Christian grace, it was thought worth inculcating by St. Paul, it is a sweetener of daily life and intercourse; it is so far like the language of heaven. Honour giving is a gospel rule, because it is a heavenly one; and so far as it goes, it brings that much of heaven upon earth.

What a society must that be, in which no jarring sound, no discourtesy of look, or deed, or word, are ever known, where all are honoured and all confer honour, where there is the refinement of delicate susceptibility; and that refinement is never shocked, that susceptibility is never hurt.

Sometimes one feels inclined to envy the thick skin, and pushing elbows, and obtuse ears which are so commonly met, because they escape so much of a refined torture—a torture which they probably never could comprehend; but let us envy not; we are more akin to the courtesy of the heavenly life and of heavenly beings, when these things so pain us that we shrink from them.

I believe that there will be something exquisite in the courtesy and grace, as well as in the love of the speech of Jesus hereafter; and His people's speech will be modelled upon His—they will then at length have caught the tones of His voice, and they shall speak after the manner of angels—yea, above the manner of angels—not in a tomb, but in the land of life.

But now we pass onward from the address of the angels, to say a word or two about the Lord Himself.

At first Jesus addressed the weeping woman in the same terms as the angels. He too said to her (γυνη) 'Woman.' We should have thought that He would at once have said 'Mary;' doubtless there are many reasons unknown to us why He did not.

But one probable reason we can see. He most likely meant to draw her out. He was about to make a great revelation to her, and He would lead her gradually up to it; just as on the journey to Emmaus He led the disciples up to that knowledge and disappearance of Himself at the breaking of bread.

We have often to be drawn out, before we can be drawn on; perhaps our sorrow has to endure a temporary aggravation before it is changed into exceeding joy. At such times we often do not know what God is doing with us, but that is the right way to blessing. We are made like the hart to pant after the water courses, before the stream which will satisfy us is revealed. God is giving us receptive power for blessing.

The Lord went further still with the angels in His address to Mary. He said as they did, "Why weepest thou?" as if He did not know all about her tears! as if He did not know that from beginning to end they were being shed for Him! He might have said, "Mary" at once; and in a moment changed her sorrow into joy; but no! He first says, 'Woman,'—and 'Woman why weepest thou?'

We should have said, perhaps, that with all the knowledge which Jesus had, this was but to mock Mary's grief; but here Jesus was speaking as elsewhere, as never other man spake; on principles which were above those of earth.

He was in truth doing that which He will ever do by each of His people in trouble—leading her unto Himself. He first led her *up* to her trouble, and then *beyond* it; first up to her sorrow, then beyond it to Himself—the One for whom she grieved.

So the blessed One does for us. He often leads us up to our trouble. He allows it for a little while to become intensified; but it is only that we may see what it really is—how great—and pass beyond it.

And where did Jesus lead her?—to the person—to His very self—there, where only her tears could be dried, and her heart once more rejoice.

It was Christ acting after what is very often His plan—Christ a leader on. And what a leader! One who carries us beyond where angels can, for it is to Himself; and none save He can reveal Himself.

So may He be to us—may we hear angel voices, and all other voices which can do us good, the voices from the head, and the voices from the feet; but may nothing satisfy our souls but His very self—the living Lord.

THE SPEECH OF JESUS SURPASSING THAT OF ANGELS.

All that the angels who sat at the head and the feet of the place where the body of Jesus had lain can say, is, "Why weepest thou?" And much as if is, all that that young man clothed in a long white garment, sitting on the right side of the sepulchre (spoken of in Mark xvi) can say is, "Be not affrighted, ye seek Jesus of Nazareth which was crucified, He is risen, He is not here, behold the place where they laid Him. But go your way, tell His disciples and Peter that He goeth before you into Galilee, there shall ye see Him as He said unto you."

"He is not here." "He is risen." "Why weepest thou?" all comforting, all beautiful, all helpful; still all, not Christ Himself; and therefore not satisfying to those who profoundly loved the very individual—the Lord Himself.

It was a grand testimony; and greatly privileged were they who were commissioned to give it, but so far did it go, and no farther.

We can easily understand its limitation by looking at what is analagous in human love. The messenger who tells us about the One we love, and bears us His message, is very valued by us; but it is upon the loved One Himself that the heart is set; messenger and message are only valuable in so far as they manifest His mind, and point to Him.

And all ministers can only go a certain length. Do their utmost, be they from heaven or earth, they can but testify of Christ—most blessed, new, and wonderful things they may tell us, as did that angel in Mark xvi, 5, but they are not Christ Himself; and therefore cannot satisfy the soul.

Angel Guarded in Death. 229

This is not without its teaching and ministry for us; for we, ever prone to cling to the instrument, and to tarry in statements of truth without going on into their realities, often are a long time before we move on into the very life and being of that which we have heard. We tarry in ministries, and sermons, and, perhaps, ministers themselves; and do not hasten on to the One testified of—to the Lord Himself.

Let us put all in their proper place. Many can tell us about Jesus—they can be as angels of God to us; but none save Jesus can reveal Himself.

And this He will ever do. He will never leave those who have heard about Him with intense longing, who cannot be satisfied apart from Him—to remain without Him. He has not said to means, "Hither shall ye go and no further," in order to make that point the extreme limit which we shall reach. He says, "After ye, then Myself."

So we may observe in passing; be careful not to misuse ministries and means—onward to the Lord Himself. Jesus has much in store for you. Jesus will have personal contact with you—onward through all—unsatisfied by all—beyond all—to Christ.

But Mary was not at once brought into immediate contact with her Lord. She was led up, and that somewhat painfully to the point of consummation; she passed through suffering on account of the crucified One, before she saw Him returned from the dead.

Now it is a matter of experience that, in almost all cases, those to whom Christ has been revealed have arrived at that revelation through many previous leadings. They have been led up to the Lord. They have been taught much about Him, before they knew Himself; they were not at peace, or satisfied while they were being led up; they were in the way of blessing, but had not attained to the high blessing itself. If these lines meet the eyes of any who are now undergoing leadings to the Lord, rather than enjoying experimental knowledge of the Lord Himself, strugglings, tears, depressions, and many such sad trials, let them be greatly comforted by the knowledge that Christ never leads up to Himself without revealing Himself. There is a consummation to all this. None but Jesus can say, 'Here I am;' none, save He, can pronounce our name with the voice which we want to hear; but He can, and as He can, so He will.

But now, let us inquire when and how the Lord gave this revelation of Himself, satisfying the thirsty soul of that woman, who had been unsatisfied by the two angels at the head and feet of the place where the body of Jesus had lain.

The holy angels were within the grave, but Jesus was outside it, in its immediate neighbourhood; for her sake at its very mouth, but outside.

Angel Guarded in Death. 231

The first revelation then of Jesus after His resurrection, contained in its very circumstances the outlines of a truth of surpassing importance to the church. The facts of those circumstances said what He Himself afterwards embodied in so many words, "I am He that liveth and was dead." They said, 'Jesus is connected with death, but is freed from it.' Mary had seen Him dead; and the Lord in one sense, would never have His connection with death broken, but it must be always as bound up with resurrection life—Jesus *and* the grave, but Jesus *outside* the grave. What a presentation was that to Mary, how real! considering all that had just passed—how new! how wonderful! how soul satisfying as regarded the present loneliness and grief!

Now, all this is ours. Jesus meets us in our weepings as the very conqueror of that which has caused our tears. Sin has separated between us and Him. He says, 'I was accounted as a sinner for you, but, lo! I have paid the penalty of sin; I am conqueror over sin and all that belongs to it; here I am alive for you.'

Do we fear death? Jesus says, 'I was dead, I have been what you must be; but my place now is outside the tomb, and so is yours—death is conquered for you.'

Jesus meets us in the place of our woe, and speaks to us as none other can.

Those were very comforting words which that

young man clothed in a long white garment spake to the women in the sepulchre, but they went out quickly and fled, they trembled and were amazed; but when Jesus spake, (truly as it was said of Him, as never other man spake,) though it was but a single word, Mary's heart responded at once in ecstasy and peace.

Surely, sad and weeping ones should be comforted when they think of Jesus, meeting in the neighbourhood of the grave the one who perseveringly for His sake was tarrying and weeping there. She too must be numbered amongst the dull and slow of heart to believe all that the prophets had spoken; but Jesus knowing her mission there, the deep occupation of her heart about Himself, does not chide her; at a grave she was tarrying, beyond a grave she could not go, and Jesus met her there.

Here, then, Jesus revealed Himself; and next, we are to ask how the revelation was made.

Had we been in Jesus' place, we should have made some great manifestation of glory—we should have encompassed ourselves with the awe which belongs to another world; we should have said, 'The one we love will be rejoiced to see me in the light and glory which belong to me'—and much like this would have passed through our minds. But it was wholly otherwise with Christ. He does manifest Himself, and that unmistakably; but then, it is as with the still small voice.

He was still man—the risen man—He knew what was in man, in the good sense as well as in the bad; He knew avenues to Mary's heart—yes, the avenue by which He is always best pleased to approach.

And so when Jesus had led Mary up to the very point of her sorrow, bringing her by the word 'Whom' to have as it were before her a perfect picture of the One she loved—a vivid likeness drawn by the very anguish of her love, He revealed Himself by a single word—and that word her own name 'Mary.' Thank God for the intense humanity of the way of revelation—for the honour it puts on humble love, for its delicacy and refinement, for the subtlety of its power.

It is indeed intensely human—and super-human too.

Few are the words which are spoken, when after a long absence those who love each other dearly meet again. At such times silence is the highest eloquence, and the quivering but unspeaking lip discards the common phraseology of human speech.

But a return after long and painful absence is not the only circumstance under which this discoursing silence proclaims the mutual feelings of the heart. It is thus also when relations and dearly loving friends meet after something has been endured, or some great trial has been passed, or some threatened evil overcome. Then, also, men seldom speak, or if they do, they utter but a name, as though the fulness of their hearts had stopped their utterance; or as though they feared that any sound would break the sweet charm in which their spirits were enchained.

Now these two circumstances we find united in the meeting of Mary and her Lord. He had been long absent from her, and now He had come back again. It is true she had been near Him when He hung upon the cross, only a few hours before, and for but a few hours He had been hidden from her sight; but hours were more than days to the Magdalene's holy love.

But it was not the time which filled this meeting with such surpassing awe; it was the place whither He had been. He had been on a journey to the unknown land. He had been in the grave. He who said to her 'Mary,' had been dead. Much had been endured, the great trial had been past, the threatened evil had been overcome; and all this was thought of, and spoken of, in the two words which passed between the Magdalene and her Lord.

Christ's way of revelation was by an appeal to Mary's own inward consciousness—to a certain fulness within—to an ineffable union which there was between herself and Him.

The power—the beauty of the method of appeal, and of the strength which it put forth instantaneously makes it to be beyond the reach of explanation by words.

It is its glory so to be—we shall not attempt to dim that glory by endeavouring to shew how the pronunciation of a name could flood a soul with light and joy.

Is not this the very thing we want ourselves? not reasons, not proofs, not arguments about divine things—about love; but the very love-bond itself. We want intense heart susceptibility and sensitiveness; we want an acute stringing of the nerves of the soul, if we may so describe it; we want to get beyond the long dull process of many words into the mystic force of the gathered-up intensity of a single word—we want the saying of our name by our blessed Lord to be enough.

Oh, dear reader, do you understand this; do you pant for it; do you long to be away beyond your grossness and heaviness of heart—are you, too, in tears and sadness? well, sooner or later, you shall hear a word, you shall feel a thrill, an electric spark shall flash into your soul—nothing new will be said—even as nothing was to Mary—but you shall know that it is *the* Lord—yes, *your* Lord that speaks to you, and calls you by your name.

This is an example of concentrated power. It was not given to the angels at the head and feet thus to speak, but only to Christ Himself. And cannot we believe how in the eternal dwelling of Jesus' people with Him, there will be many such revelations of Himself as were here given by the

Lord to Mary. Then we shall be in a fit state to receive them; we shall be susceptible; we shall be alive to every breathing—even one word from Christ may be a soul's feast for many a year, if eternity may be spoken of after the manner of time.

But though we cannot tell all the thoughts which now passed through Mary's mind—or anything at all with reference to some of them; we can imagine a part of what that voice pronouncing her name declared.

When Jesus said 'Mary,' it was as much as to say—'As I was, so I am—as I knew you when living, so I know you now; I am not changed to you; you are the same to me as you ever were.' Jesus bound the past and present together, when he called that weeping woman simply by her name.

In eternity there shall assuredly be such precious bindings. We shall then have a very glorious Christ in our present, but He shall be the same Christ as we had in our past—the One who bore with all our infirmities, who healed us of all our sins, who spake to us as never other man spake, or could speak. The Christ of our days of strength, and glory, and wealth, shall be the same as the Christ of our days of weakness, and sorrow, and poverty; and it would be a terrible deprivation if He were any other.

No, we shall want no new Christ in heaven, other than He whom we knew in our strivings and hard pilgrimage on earth—we are happy in the thought that we shall associate Him with a past—a past in which there is naught for us to glory, but everything for Him—we shall say "Unto Him that loved us, *and washed us from our sins in His own blood;* and hath made us kings and priests unto God and His Father—to Him be glory and dominion for ever and ever. Amen."

THE SITTING POSTURE OF THE ANGELS AT THE HEAD AND FEET OF THE PLACE WHERE THE BODY OF JESUS HAD LAIN.

Here, in the quiet of the grave, in the place of which the utmost that could be said was that, 'here the body of Jesus had lain,' the angels of God are fulfilling their appointed mission. They are not out away in the wonders of the resurrection, of which so far as the spiritual world was concerned, we may be sure there were many; they are in a place from which the interest has apparently departed; and there they are sitting, in calm and unexcited performance of their duty.

There is a comfortable thought connected with the fact of that calm sitting and performance of duty, after the departure of the body. It speaks to us and says, "You need not fear that God has not those who will tarry with and minister to you in the time of left joys."

We think when such and such a dear one is gone, or when such a sweet occupation is ended, when we are left in the place itself, but that which made the place what it was is taken away, we shall be utterly desolate. We say, we know of none who will come and minister to us; and if we did, we are not sure that they would be suited to us.

Now the presence of these calm sitting angels in the tomb, shows us that God can suit us in our hour of deprivation. Who but He could have answered the question, 'what will be a suitable vision for a weeping woman looking into an empty tomb?' and suppose the question to be answered, who but He could have sent the only suitable ones thither?

This is a thought for our own daily life; it says to us, 'Do not be utterly dismayed at the prospect of emptiness, desolation, left joys, broken centres of life, and so forth. At the head and feet may be found sitting the messengers of God—and all so calm when we are so excited, so compassing the fulness of our grief, its head and feet.

It may be that, some earthly friends will be to us then as the angels of God. Such have been thus. God has put this high honour on them, and perhaps, we ourselves have been made as the angels of God to some one; unawares this great honour was put upon us; but God has messengers not in the flesh at all—secret inspirations, visible to us, though not to others, whose high mission it is to be tarriers in the tomb. The tomb was bad enough to Mary; the empty tomb would be worse; it was completed desolation; there, amid completed desolation, angels sat. Let us remember all this in the day of our loneliness, when even a fresh surprise of sorrow comes upon us, as it did on Mary.

But let us return to the thought of the angels not being abroad in the outside wonders of this season, whatever they may have been. They are sitting in the tomb.

We have here given us a glimpse of service on a heavenly rule. It is said by the poet, that 'they also serve, who only stand and wait;' a similar thought meets us here. Obedience, contentment, repose, all come beautifully before us here. Surely these are characteristics of heavenly service, elements in heavenly happiness. If there were more of these in our service, there would be more of heaven in it too. Our imagination cannot conceive the intense action for which these angels were ready at a moment's notice; perhaps it as much fails in realizing their present position of rest.

If we look at our own past service, how sadly we have failed in these very points—our waywardness as to what should be done, and how it should be done! our dissatisfaction often as to the part assigned to us! our fussiness! or excitability! our inability to stay long in places of retirement, or of unobtrusive service! how do the remembrances of all these shame us! May we have grace to look into the tomb and contemplate these angels—may we look at them full of heavenly grace and power, sitting at the head and feet of the place where a dead body had been, where nothing was now—may we learn from the very mystery which hangs around that empty space. For many is the task which we are set by God, in His omnipotent disposal of us, which seems as barren and profitless as this, but with it we have one only concern, 'has it been commanded to us?' have we, like Philip, been directed to arise and go to a place which is desert?—the command is everything.

The glimpse of service on a heavenly rule, shews us angels not only smiting with the sword, but sitting contentedly in a tomb. 'Self' had no place in them—they were performing this service on rule; and it is the want of this which mars so much of our service here. The service itself is well meant, and all we do is well meant also; but 'self' comes into it, and brings disorder with it.

Much these angels knew was going on outside, but it was not appointed to them to be engaged in it; and we shrink from the absurd idea of their wanting so to be, or from that of their leaving their post curiously to peer into the outer world, and at least see what was going on. It surely is not a lesson without its use to us, telling us to be content to know that there are great things in which we are not to have a part—into which our place and duty are such, as to forbid us to look. If we all had such heaven-ordered minds, what peace and power would be found in a now distracted church.

From these sitting angels, let us gather also a corrective for our ideas.

We should doubtless have thought them better employed in going hither and thither to comfort this disciple and that—such would have been fit angelic work—did not an angel comfort Hagar and Elijah, and the Lord Himself? but the Lord of angels had set them there. His thoughts are not as our thoughts, nor His ways as ours. The alabaster box often has a use different from what we would appoint to it—obedience is better than sacrifice.

Let us firmly believe that God is the best judge of His own work. He will always be most honoured by our being in the place where He put us—in the book of the Rev. (xix, 17) we have an angel standing in the sun, here we have two angels sitting in a tomb.

Note, too, that in high service we have great calm—the calm proceeding from the certainty of divine commission. That was what gave Abraham calm in the sacrifice of Isaac, what gave it to Jeremiah (chap. xxvi) when he testified to all the princes and people, and said, "As for me, I am in your hand; do with me as seemeth good and meet unto you"—to Shadrach, Meshach, and Abednego, when they stood before Nebuchadnezzar—to the Apostles, when brought before the council. Christ's own calm was founded in the knowledge that He was executing the commission of the Father. The sweet feeling that we are sustaining the best part —the most proper one, and therefore the best, will give us the greatest calm.

Yet another teaching. If angels, with all their great capacities, were thus appointed to waiting service, how much more reasonable is it that we should be with our small. Some of us, poor feeble creatures as we are, think ourselves too big for this and that; as though it were not much even to be a watchman, and to be able to answer, "What of the night?"

Now one more. Sitting there, the Lord brought to those angels their work—a sorrowing woman makes her appearance—one woman met by two angels. And now what this says to us is very comforting. The Lord will bring to all waiters in service their work—their proper, best work.

When we are told to go forth, we shall find our work abroad, as many angels did in Scripture history—when we are told to abide still in our place, we shall find our work come to us. Sit still where you are placed by God—lie still, if you must lie; behold, God will bring to you that particular work which He has for you to do.

CHAPTER XIII.

THE FEET OF JESUS THE PLACE OF WORSHIP.

"And as they went to tell his disciples, behold, Jesus met them, saying, All hail. And they came and held him by the feet, and worshipped him. Then said Jesus unto them, Be not afraid: go tell my brethren that they go into Galilee, and there shall they see me."—MATT. xxviii, 9, 10.

KRUMMACHER may well attribute to that saying in John xx, 17 "a depth of meaning which has never yet been explored by man." There Jesus says to Mary, "Touch me not for I am not yet ascended to my Father; but go to my brethren and say unto them, I ascend unto my Father and your Father, and to my God, and your God."

But a very short period had elapsed since the positive prohibition to Mary to touch Him, and now we find no hindrance put in the way of these disciples; they hold Him by the feet and worship Him.

The events of the forty days after the resurrection are very full of mystery—more so than any period in our Lord's life; the forty days' temptation in the wilderness alone coming near them in this respect; and amid these mysteries we must number the fulness of meaning in this prohibition to Mary. None, we may imagine, if imagination might have any place here, would the Lord have been better pleased to allow to touch Him than this one to whom He had been so gracious, and whom He loved so well; but to her came the decided prohibition, "Touch me not."

In a work like this, which makes no profession of criticism, this subject presents some difficulty. For it must be so treated as to be drawn into harmony with the general tone of the book in which it finds place; and at the same time the reader should receive some information on it, other than would be at his disposal from its simple spiritual teachings.

The best plan, then, to adopt, will be to gather together in a condensed form something of what others have said on this matter; and then to present the reader with such spiritual teachings as have been suggested to our own minds.

We could not pass by some consideration of this refusal of Mary's touch; because one of the first questions which would suggest itself to the mind on reading this touching by the disciples in the passage before us, would be, "Why were they allowed to touch, and why was she forbidden?"

The Place of Worship.

Steir truly says the difficulty lies in the rigorously literal idea of the word "touch," which we must certainly hold fast; and in the obscure connection of the reason given in the word "for." All expositions which sacrifice the one or the other are to be rejected. Thus, the prohibition to "touch," must first be taken literally.*

Why then did our Lord not permit Mary to touch Him?

The answer to this question will be best given by proposing another, *i.e.*, In what spirit, and for what purpose did Mary want to touch? Was it to satisfy curiosity? Was it to dispel doubt?

We cannot well imagine the mere feeling of curiosity, however natural to Mary as a woman, finding any place in such a scene as this. It was not out of curiosity—nor yet out of doubt. For Mary had no doubt as to this being her very Lord. As Steir says, " In this Rabboni is breathed her whole soul, the conscious and inexpressibly comfort-

---

* Steir mentions several extraordinary interpretations, *e.g.*, "Make thyself not unclean, by touching one who has been buried" (Wetstein). Schleiermacher reproduced a rationalistic notion which here and there finds unaccountable acceptance, that the new life of the newly risen Lord was as yet too tenderly susceptible to be touched. Paulus conceived that the Lord went into the garden with His wounds as yet unsoothed. According to Brennecke, He said, "My body unprotected, everything pains me; I have not yet died, but shall die." According to Venturini, "Touch Me not yet, this afflicted body remains yet susceptible to pain; the wounds which the reckless inflicted upon Me, torment Me still." &c., &c.

ing return to her earlier fellowship with the Teacher and Master, on whose lips her ear and her heart had hung. This full and decisive Rabboni had no half questioning tone in it, as if followed by a note of interrogation. After such a call as this there could follow nothing but a full recognition, there was no room for the doubtful, 'Art Thou then truly He?' Moreover the words, 'I am not yet ascended,' could have had no bearing on this. And again, if doubt was prominent in Mary's mind the Lord would not have been able to say, 'Touch me not for I am He, and thy touching is not necessary,' but rather must, as in Luke xxiv, 39, have challenged her to the touch in order to invigorate her confidence. For it could do Him no offence, and wherefore then might she not touch Him? As in the case before us, He does not deter the women from 'holding Him by the feet,' but uttered an encouraging 'be not afraid;' and He Himself requires the apostles in the evening, and Thomas afterwards actually to touch Him."

The Lord's repelling word is a sublime and profound declaration—" *No, thus it was not designed* "—enforced from Him by the opposition between the heavenly feeling of His own mind, and the earthly feeling of Mary's spirit. It is as though He said, " Sensible experience and apprehension will avail no more from this time. Thou wilt not possess and hold and enjoy my presence as thou didst before My death." Did not Mary betray that thought and feeling by the "Rabboni," a word entirely derived from their former relation, but which as spoken to Him, and addressing Him by His title as Teacher, is in strange contrast with the "Lord" addressed to the Gardener, and the "my Lord" to men and angels.

The idea of Mary, then, being that she was to have her Lord, even as He had been to her before, Jesus had to meet that mistaken thought, and He does so at the fittest time, and in the best way.

Jesus had spoken marvellously to this favoured woman when He uttered her name—the simple word "Mary." He had come near her with an inward living voice and thrill, and now He immediately retreats from her again, for she interprets humanly what He interprets divinely; she in an earthly, but He in a heavenly sense. It is as though He said, "The relation between us is somewhat changed; my former life with you will return no more, but after a brief time of transition my elevation to the Father will come—all this from the beginning thou must know and ponder well."

Dr. Hannah has put this matter with his usual lucidity in his volume on the Forty days after the Resurrection. He says that, "it cannot be supposed that the mere object of affording proof enough that He was still alive, would have detained Jesus here so long. That could have been done in two days as well as forty. Besides had that been the object of His delay, why did He not appear oftener in a more open and public manner than He did? Neither can it be imagined that it was for the purpose of continued and enlarged intercourse with His disciples. The fewness and shortness of the interviews with them precludes that belief. He is seen by them but ten times in all .... and what impression was all this studied distance and reserve to make upon the minds of His disciples? Put yourself into their exact position at this time: remember that not one* of them before His death had risen to any thought or belief in His divinity—that from all their earlier earthly notions of Him they had to be weaned; that after days and years of the easiest companionship with Him, they had to be raised to the belief that it was the very Lord of heaven and earth with whom they had been holding converse; yet that belief was to be so formed within them as not to militate against the idea of His true and proper humanity. See, then, what an important part in the execution of this needful but most difficult task, must have been fulfilled by His mode of dealing with them during the forty days."

"For, let us only conceive what should have

* We are unable here to enter into such statements as those in John ix, 35—38; Matt. xvi, 16; John xi, 27; and desire to quote the above admirable and lucid extract, subject to whatever the fulness or power of such statements may have been. P.

happened if one or other of the two alternatives had been realized: if at once, after a few interviews, sufficient simply to do away with all doubt as to His resurrection, Jesus had passed up into the heavens, never to be seen again on earth; let us imagine that the descent of the Spirit had immediately thereon ensued; that the day of Pentecost had followed immediately on the day of the resurrection; that the eyes of the apostles had thus at once and fully been enlightened, and the great truth of their Master's Godhead had flashed upon their minds; the danger would undoubtedly have been, that, seen in the blaze of that new glory, shining thus around His person, the man Christ Jesus had been lost, and the humanity swallowed up in the divinity: nor would it have been so easy to persuade those men that, ascended up on high, seated at the right hand of the Father, He was the same Jesus still;—a brother to them as truly as when He lived among them, equally alive to all human sympathies as when He walked with them by the way, or sat down with them in the upper chamber.

"Take again the other alternative; that after His resurrection Christ had immediately resumed and continued—even let us say for no longer a time than these forty days—the exact kind of life that He had led before, returning to all His old haunts and occupations and . . . . would not such a return on His part to all the old familiarities of

His former intercourse have had a tendency to check the rising faith in His divinity; to tie His disciples down again to a knowledge of Him only after the flesh; to give to the humanity of the Lord such bulk and prominence as to make it in their eyes overshadow the divinity? Can you conceive a treatment more nicely fitted to the spiritual condition, to the spiritual wants of those men at that time, than the very one which the Lord adopted and carried out—so well fitted as it was, gradually, gently, without violence, (as is ever the mode of His actions in all the provinces of His spiritual empire) to lead those disciples on from their first misty, imperfect, unworthy ideas of His person, character, and work, on and up to clearer, purer, loftier conceptions of Him? In what better way could a faith in their Master's divinity have been superinduced upon their former faith in Him as a man, a friend, a brother, so that the two might blend together without damage done to either by the union; their knowledge of Him as human, not interfering with their trust in Him as divine, their faith in Him as God, not weakening their attachment to Him as man.

With this key in our hand—a key which unlocks much of the mystery of our Lord's conduct throughout those forty days—let us return to Mary in the garden. She sees Jesus alive once more before her. She hears Him, as of old, call her by her name; He is hers, she thinks, again—hers as He had been before; hers not to be torn from her again. All the warmth of those former days of familiar friendship filling her glad heart, she offers Him not the homage of a higher worship, but addresses Him as He did her; "Raboni," she says —my own, my old, my well-loved Master. She makes some gesture as of embracing him. Gently, but firmly our Lord repels the too warm, too human, too familiar approach. "Touch me not, Mary. You think of me as given back to be to you the same exactly that I was before. You are mistaken; our relationship is changed; our method of intercourse must be altered. You must learn to think of me and to act towards me differently from what you ever did before; I am here, but it is only for a short season; I am on earth, but I am now on my way to my Father; my home is no longer with you and the others here below, it is there with my Father, up in heaven; still shall I feel to you and all the others as tenderly as I ever felt, not ashamed to call them even still my brethren. Touch me not, then, Mary; stop not to lavish on me an affection that has in it too much of the human, too little of the divine; but go to my brethren, and say unto them, 'I ascend to my Father, and to your Father, and to my God and to your God; my Father and my God in a sense in which He is not and cannot be yours; but your Father and your God in a sense in which He could not have been yours had I not died and risen, and been on my way now to sit down with Him on the throne of glory in the heavens."

We see, then, that there were good reasons why Mary should not be allowed to touch the Lord; but no such reasons existed in the case of these women. They were in the act of fulfilling the commission given to them by the angels, when He met them with greeting, saying, 'All hail.' It was the same Jesus who thus acted so differently, forbidding even a touch to one; and permitting what might be called a long holding to others.

The like happens continually now in the intercourse between Jesus and His people.

It is the same Christ who acts, but the actings are in opposite directions. Sometimes we stumble at this. We measure what He does by *our* slight knowledge of people's circumstances, feelings, dangers, temptations, we think we know what indeed is only known to Him. We may be certain that in every instance there is a nice adaptation to the individual need. The permitting to one may seem very large, and the withholding to another very strict; and, moreover, we may think that the one from whom a heart's desire is withheld, is the very one to whom it should be given; but let us say, 'It is the Lord, shall He not do as He will with His own, shall He not act out of the fulness of His own knowledge, both as regards us and the interests of His kingdom?'

Jesus thus dealt differently with people who

seemed apparently to be in much the same position. They all loved Him, they were all bereft, they were all disciples. But the sameness of position is very often only apparent, there is fundamental difference. We may safely leave it to Jesus how to treat the case of each disciple and lover.

And is it not a great comfort to know that He will discriminate? What should become of us if He did not—how exalted some would become, how set in slippery places; and how depressed others, how cast into gloom.

All things here seem jumbled up together; but with Him and in His dealings with us, there will be fine discrimination.

Only let us make sure that it is 'the Lord' with whom we have to do; and that point secured, all will be well.

We perceive, too, that there is that permitted (because it could be done so harmlessly) to those in the way of active duty, which may be dangerous to one whose soul is simply filled with feeling.

Steir, in his exposition of the words of Jesus, is very strong upon the command given to Mary, "But go to my brethren, and say unto them, I ascend unto my Father, and your Father, and to my God and to your God." "The chief thing is for thee *the going*, and for me *the ascending*. Understand, then, my manifestation aright, and make good thy first sad tidings of an empty sepulchre." "The Lord requires of us all that we should not find our rest in the sensuous sentiment of moments of sweet communion with Him, not seek, as it were, to touch Him in love too much mingled with selfish ingredients, but *go forth* with our commission into life, to do the work for which He sends us.*

Indeed this holding thus permitted to these women while in the activity of a high ministry, even the bearing of a message of the resurrection to the disciples, occupies a particularly safe and happy place. It is preceded by an "All hail;" it is followed by a "Be not afraid." It was made safe to them by the position in which it was vouchsafed, and by the command to them to proceed in the mission on which they were. To them this privilege might have been no more safe than to Mary, had not the command to up and speed upon their way been quickly given. It is the balance of the Christian life—we are not constructed for communion without activity, nor for activity without communion—the mingling of the two is Christian life. David connected them then together, "I will run the way of thy commandments when thou shalt enlarge my heart."

We see here, also, one of the surprises of the

* Lange's note quoted is both interesting and suggestive. He denies the touching to Mary alone, to shew, on the one hand, that she surpassed all the rest, even the men in faith, and was so fully assured of the resurrection, that she needed no further confirmation; and on the other hand, to teach how those who surpass others in faith will find it necessary to demonstrate and approve its strength in the absence of nearer communion with their Lord.

spiritual life. There are such, even as in the life natural. What could be such a joyful surprise as this appearance of the Saviour to the disciples on the road? Surely the spiritual life is not the dull and uneventful one which some suppose. The people of the world look upon it as one of monotony, with no events, no changes, no pleasures, no healthy excitements—but it is because they do not know it. No doubt it has its alternations from joy to sorrow, but also those from sorrow to joy— if there are heavy days for Zion when her children sit down by the waters of Babylon and weep, there are others where the Lord, having turned their captivity, they are like unto them that dream.

We are reminded also of the blessed confirmations which there are in the spiritual life. The angel's words, "He is not here, he is risen," are assured as true to them by the Lord Himself. It was the highest confirmation which they could get.

The wonders which the Samaritan woman told her people, were attested by the Saviour, so that they believed, not because of her word, but because of the confirmation which they received with their own ears. And, surely, amongst His dealings of blessing with His people, this confirmation is not to be forgotten. We hear from ministers, we read in books, this and that good thing about Him; who can confirm them to us like Himself?

If we simply believe, (however much amazed and confused we may be)—and obey—for being found in the path of obedience is everything, our faith shall receive confirmation. It may be in an unlikely and unexpected way, but it will be in God's way. God has His own confirmations for those who are in the path of active faith, as suitable to us at the particular time and under our particular circumstances—as wonderful, as gracious as this permission to the women to hold the Saviour by the feet and worship Him.

CHAPTER XIV.

THE FEET OF JESUS THE PLACE OF COMFORT.

"*And when he had thus spoken, he shewed them his hands and his feet.*"—LUKE xxiv, 40.

WE have seen the Lord prohibit a touch in the case of Mary, and permit it in the case of those whom He met in the way, and who fell at His feet and worshipped Him; now we see Him even offering Himself to the touch of all who were gathered together in that guarded chamber, saying: "Behold my hands and my feet that it is I myself; handle me and see, for a spirit hath not flesh and bones, as ye see me have. And when he had thus spoken, he shewed them his hands and his feet."

We can easily in some degree imagine the terror of these disciples at this sudden apparition of their Lord.

The terrible and wonderful events of the last few days, following each other in such quick succession—the strange matters unaccounted for, and unaccountably connected with the resurrection—had left them in anything but a favourable condition for the reception of their Lord with any degree of calmness, coming as He did in so mysterious a way.

There has been much controversy as to the Lord's entrance through the door—as to the nature of His body, and as to how He entered. Some think He knocked and was given admittance, some that He entered immediately after the Emmaus disciples, before the door was again shut; but the whole tone and words of the narrative point to a silent, sudden manifestation of Himself—"He stood in the midst."

Connected with these speculations as to how the Lord entered the room, are others connected with the nature of His body. We need not for our purpose enter upon these: we shall content ourselves with two or three remarks of Steir's, from which it will be seen of what nature that body probably was, and why in probability it thus came.

"To the intervening condition of the forty days, as the Scripture exhibits it, there corresponds nothing but a medium between perfect spiritualization or glorification, and perfect similarity to the state before death. All our error may be traced to an unhappy leaning either to the one or the other of these extremes."

Then, as to Christ thus appearing in a miraculous way. "He will teach His disciples two things—that He lives bodily, and that His bodiliness, to obviate all misunderstanding, is at the same time different, and already less bound than before. . . . We must leave all exact definition, and confine ourselves, on a subject of which we know nothing, to the simple truth that the Lord, as He could be either visible or invisible, so could come into a closed room—that this was a miracle connected with the relatively miraculous nature of His present body; and that St. John records it as and because the Lord did it—to indicate this characteristic of His risen body."

Let us now take up a few thoughts of practical teaching and comfort for ourselves.

Observe here, one calm One, and many agitated ones; and the calm One ministering out of Himself to the agitated ones. Such is the picture presented to us here, and the like is often re-produced in the church, and in individual souls. If we could have seen the horror-stricken countenances of the apostles and disciples, and the calm, sweet look of Christ, these would have taught us more than all that could be written on the subject.

The church is privileged to rejoice in the presence of an ever calm, collected Lord. Conscious of His power, and dignity, and feelings, and of what He is, and what we are, He is ever calm—not uninterested, but unexcited; not nervous, yet not nerveless; above all agitations, but not above feeling for those who are subject to them.

We accept this picture as a typical one; we

would realize it in all the agitations and weaknesses, and affrights of our spiritual, yea, and even our temporal life. In all our agitations, our soul will crave the presence of some calm one on whom we may lean. Our own friends and relatives will very possibly not supply the want at all—and even if they do in some measure, that 'some' will not be enough. We shall have to go deeper than they; we shall have to hear Jesus saying, 'Look at me.'

And how is it that Jesus ministers to our fears? When the disciples were in the boat tossed with waves, and He came to them, and they thought it to be a spirit, He said, "It is I, be not afraid;" and now He says here, "It is I, myself."

Surely it would be a wonderful sight, if we could see Jesus thus ministering now—revealing Himself, His intense reality, His human sympathy and feelings to multitudes of fearful ones here and there. In Himself He contains a well-spring of peace and comfort enough for all. He would have us, at all these times, still our souls with a deep and thorough consciousness that it is His very self with whom we have to do, "Behold my hands and my feet," He "shewed unto them his hands and his feet."

It was by this manifestation that the Lord set right the *thoughts* which had arisen in the hearts of this terrified company. Their "thoughts" had reference doubtless to that which they saw before them, but could not understand. There is

The Place of Comfort.

no reason to suppose that they thought that this was any other than Jesus, or that they were not aware that it actually was Jesus; but then what was He exactly, appearing under these strange circumstances? They evidently thought Him to be a spirit—not a phantasma as in Matt. xiv, 26, but the actual Lord Himself, only without a body.

The disciples believed that it was Jesus, but one different from their own well-known Jesus.

Now the Lord meant to reassure them—to shew them that He was not pure spirit—that He was His very self, and consequently their very own.

For these two thoughts are bound together; if He shewed them that He was His very self, He would at the same time shew them that He was their very own. The tie between them had been broken only so far as death could break it, and now Jesus shews that death's doings have been undone, so He gives ocular demonstration—He shews them "his hands and his feet."

These were pierced—and it was the will of Christ that He should present Himself to His disciples, even as He does to all now, as " the crucified."

It was in relation to Him as the crucified that they were to stand for the future—for ever—they, in common with the whole church; the proof therefore which He condescends to give in the first case is the exhibition of the marks of crucifixion.

It is thus, indeed, that Jesus wills ever to be

recognized. αὐτὸς ἐγώ εἰμι—(autos ego eimi), "Not merely," says Steir, "I am He Myself," but it absolutely connects His new life with His previous well known life. "I am indeed the same that was with you before death, it is my whole human personality, and not merely as a spirit."

The disciples have now to comprehend and take in the idea of their Lord's new and risen life, but as a life bound up with the past. And thus it is to be with us. The new, the resurrection, the ascension life of Jesus is ours; but in all our graspings after realizing it, we must steadily keep in view the old life—its trials and its cross.

Surely the crucified feet should be to us, at least, who can calmly look back upon the whole history of Jesus, the best exposition of the present glory of the feet burning like unto fine brass, as though they burned in a furnace. All the explanations which we shall have throughout eternity of the Lord will be connected with His piercings. The many crowns which are on His head are all linked to the many piercings of that one crown of thorns which the soldiers plaited, and with which they mockingly adorned His brow.

"It is I Myself," said Jesus; and then immediately there comes the showing of the wounds. Oh what a stilling to all heart fear—'He and His wounds'—Oh blessed thought that henceforth He never can be separated from those wounds!

So presents He Himself to all of us, so would

He have us present Him to all others—saying to them, " It is He Himself—behold His hands and His feet."

And when thoughts arise in our hearts—as from time to time they will—fears, and qualms, and surmisings, and doubtings, coming unbidden, coming we know not whence, brooding thoughts, disturbing thoughts—thoughts impossible to grasp, which by their very shadowy nature terrify us, or depress us—then, for these, Christ has for all time provided an antidote in the incident which we have been considering now — against all such thoughts He presents something solid—so solid that even our gross natures need require no more: —He speaks—He shews—He says, " It is I myself," He shews His hands and His feet.

CHAPTER XV.

THE FEET OF JESUS THE PLACE OF MANIFESTED GLORY.

" And his feet like unto fine brass, as if they burned in a furnace."—REV. I, 15.

AT length we come to a vision of the Lord Jesus Christ, in manifest, unclouded, and perfect glory.

We have seen Him wayfaring in Judæa, lying in a grave, and giving to His people but fitful glances of Himself after His resurrection—but now He is manifested in fulness of light.

It is true this manifestation is of but partial use to us; for as yet we can but little understand anything of His great glory; but what little we can gather up and comprehend, is of great value. That vision of the once travel-stained, but now effulgent feet, may be very helpful to us even in what remains to us of our pilgrimage through the dusty paths of life.

The glory manifested to us here is very magnificent. It is as complete as grand. It presents Christ from head to foot. In the midst of the seven candlesticks is "One like unto the Son of man, clothed with a garment down to the foot, and girt about the paps with a golden girdle. His head and His feet are white like wool, as white as snow; and His eyes are as a flame of fire. His feet are like unto fine brass, as if they burned in a furnace. His voice is as the sound of many waters; in His right hand are seven stars; out of His mouth proceeds a sharp two-edged sword; and His countenance is as the sun shining in its strength." Was it any marvel that when John saw Him, he fell at His feet as dead?

Apart from the consideration of who it is that embodies in Himself this glory, such a sight could have but one effect upon man, and that is repulsion. All that the beholder could say, is: "Woe is me, for I am a man of unclean lips—Woe is me, for I have seen the Lord in his glory;" but that gracious act of the Glorious One—His laying His right hand upon John, and saying, 'Fear not'— His telling him who He was; not only that He was the First and the Last, but that He was the One that liveth and was dead, and is now alive for evermore, brings him and us, who would contemplate this glory along with him, into a new position altogether.

This sight is no longer one of repulsion, but of attraction. Jesus binds heaven and earth together —binds them for us in the only way in which they can be bound—in the bond of connection made by

Himself—the One who has been on earth, who is in heaven.

This glory, then, of Jesus, we must look at, not as repellent, but as attractive—not as that with which we have nothing to do, as being immeasurably beyond us, but as that with which we have the highest interest. For if Jesus be ours, is not this the beauty of *our* Christ? Have not we a connection with Him, which makes His glory to be dear to us, even as our sufferings are dear to Him?

Moreover, we can never look at Him without learning. All this book of Revelation is for teaching. "Blessed," it says in verse 3, "is he that readeth," and that blessing belongs to him who considers the feet burning like brass, as well as to the searchers into the prophecy of that which was to be.

We have already, it is to be hoped, learned something from considering the feet of the Lord on earth, and in the tomb, and as risen from that tomb. We cannot but hope for teaching from the consideration of them in heaven. As a mere abstract sight, the revelation which we have here of Him is wonderful, but its value consists in its connection with ourselves.

First then, let us gather up some thoughts from the feet of Jesus being in glory at all.

This picture is in all particulars that of a man. A provision is here made for the manifestation of the unbroken humanity of the Lord—as a man He walked the earth, as such He is in heaven. He had walked amongst men, as a man, before His death; as a man He died and was buried; after resurrection He expressly asserted His manhood, pointing out that a spirit had not flesh and bones, as the disciples saw that He had—thus He ascended, and thus now is He seen by St. John in glory.

The believer should admit in thought no break in the manhood of his Lord. We should keep Jesus before us in that wondrous connection with us to which it pleased the Father that He should condescend; if we do not, we shall find two evils come upon us, one weakening for the present, and another, clouding for the future.

The believer derives his present power from union with a Christ who walked sinlessly an evil earth—from One who felt sorrow, and pain, and want, as he does himself; and if that Christ have gone away to heaven, where such things can be no more, and have left His manhood, and manhood's feelings behind Him, where is the tried believer to look for that sympathy upon which it is so essential that he should lean?

The natural tendency of the mind would be not to connect glory and human nature together—to think that when earth is ended with, that which is human should be left behind; but God knows that we need human sympathies in our High Priest, and there they are in the man Christ Jesus, with full manhood in heaven.

No man can be a strong believer, a strong sufferer, a strong actor, who does not gather his strength, be it with more or less of consciousness, from the presence of the man Christ Jesus in glory.

Moreover: if we know nothing of Christ in this light, the connection between the present and the future is far less real for us than it ought to be—than God has made it—we are making ourselves other than what God has done.

God does not will that we should lose ourselves as men in dreamy thoughts of a glory and a future connected some way with a spirit life. He never made us to be simply spirit—or intended us to have a simple spirit prospect before us; therefore, when He presents before us in glory, and thereof in consummation the man Christ Jesus, it is as a man still.

Surely it is as such we expect to see Him, and to be with Him, and to think of Him evermore.

No doubt there is a great difference between the aspect which Jesus presented to St. John in glory, and that which He did when the beloved apostle lay upon His breast, but the essential nature of the Lord was unchanged.

Yes! Christ's preserved manhood in glory tells us not to want to make ourselves other than what God has designed us to be. Some talk as though

Place of Manifested Glory.

heaven were the getting rid of all that belongs to manhood and the like; they talk of so-and-so being an angel, and of glorified spirits; but did Jesus get rid of manhood? and what can we aim at higher than what He is? Not one amongst the angels will hereafter equal glorified man, of whom the head is the Son of God (both God and man) Himself.

The interest which we have in heaven is not only on account of Godhead, but manhood.

When our business lies in insisting on, arguing for, or unfolding one side of a truth, we are very apt to be taxed by unthinking people with denying its other side. So it may be well to guard ourselves against any misconception by stating the fulness of our belief in the essential Godhead of Jesus, and His oneness with the Father—very God of very God—begotten, not made. But that truth fully stated, our chief concern lies with the human side of His being—His human nature in glory.

We have a distinct interest in heaven, not only because of the presence of the Father there, and of the Son in His Godhead, but on account of the Son in His manhood.

Christ Himself develops this class of interest by the particular manifestation which He here gives of Himself. Nothing is detracted from the glory of His Godhead—that remains as grand as ever; and how much is unfolded of His manhood!

Does God will us to have an interest in heaven—in Christ as there now, on account of manhood? Yes; for man was very dear to Him.

Our original redemption proved this—the whole bent of God's mind towards us proved it; if we want to know how dear man was to God, we have only to look at His Son as a man in glory.

The feet of Jesus as a man pierced and fixed to the cross have a teaching for us on this head, as on earth; the feet of Jesus glorious like unto fine brass, have the same for us as from heaven.

This particular manifestation of our Lord shows us further, that it is the Father's will that manhood should not be separated from His Son. They cannot be so separated for ever. Jesus has taken upon Himself the human nature for eternity. The idea wrought out in death, resurrection, and ascension, was not to get rid of it, but to exalt it, as we see by this manifestation of it in glory.

God does not will us to deny our nature; He made us men, and He means us to continue men for ever; how great, then, our interest in humanity glorified in heaven!

Surely this ought to make heaven and glory more real to us; it ought to make our ideas and our hopes more definite than they are; it ought to make us more earnest in striving to be holy as men. Instead of connecting the future with being rid of the nature which God has given us, and in which it is His will that He shall be eternally praised and glorified, we shall desire Him to be glorified in it now, as much as can be on the earth, and we shall look forward to glorifying Him in it for ever. This will animate us as men; this will make our daily human life real; this will keep us from those strange and dreamy notions which from their very undefinedness help to weaken the influence which the other life should have on this.

It is true St. Paul desired to be delivered from the body of this death, and now we groan being burdened; but all that we would be rid of, are the sorrow, and pain, and burden, and decay, which belong to sin; human nature, and the human form glorified, await us hereafter.

For observe next:

This drawing near, this drawing in of manhood to God, is shewn to us very clearly by Christ's appearance as a man in glory. He is there as our representative head, and He would be no representative, if He had after ascension entered a phase of being altogether different from ours. Therefore we learn two things from this magnificent appearance of Christ—one is, that God wills to have man very close to Himself, and the other, that He will have him very exalted.

There was a terrible going out from God in the case of the first man, Adam—there is a glorious drawing in by the second man, Jesus Christ. And should not this dispel a whole host of fears and doubts as to God's good will concerning us? When we feel human nature in its weakness, and short coming, and decay, should we not look away from what we feel in ourselves, to what are the great intentions of God? Should we not see that whatever may be our weakness, it shall not countervail His strength? Shall not we, who are one with Christ by God's own way of faith, behold Him passed through His sufferings to glory, and believe that we shall be brought triumphantly and safely through ours?

Jesus, for the joy that was set before Him, endured the cross, despising the shame; and when we think of the capacities of our human nature—of the drawing near of it to God by and by, let us bear with whatever may be our lot here. Let us refuse to be down-pressed beyond measure; let us spring at the thought of the possibilities which exist for the very nature in which we are suffering.

And let us seek now, and here. It was in human nature that Jesus was holy—it was to Him as in human nature that Satan came, and had nothing in Him—it was as man He hungered and thirsted, and men tried to make him a king, and people sought to entangle Him in His talk; and now in that very victorious nature He is glorified in heaven. Surely it will be helpful to us, if we say, 'as a man, I am to be with God for ever, therefore as a man will I seek after being holy now.'

We have already spoken of the power of contrast in the mind of the Lord Jesus Christ; now this idea of contrast comes in again. There it was the contrast between suffering and ministration, between execrations and Hosannahs,—here it is the opposite; between glory and shame—rest and weariness—the light of burning brass, the dust stain of travel.

We must fix our eyes again upon the manhood of the Son of God. This is the aspect of man in glory before God; contrasted, yet connected with His aspect on earth—the same man in both instances—the man Christ Jesus.

These are the very feet which were sorely weary, which were dust stained, which were pierced, which needed and accepted human ministration; and now they are like unto fine brass, as if they burned in a furnace. What a contrast to the Lord himself! *The* past—*His* past will never be effaced from His mind—no, not the smallest incident of it; and contrast will work by the law of its own nature, and will call up in Him all the thoughts which properly belong to it.

And there is another who remembers all the past, *i.e.*, the Father. All things are remembered of Christ by Him. And *why* they were so is remembered also. All the humiliation and suffering of the Son is connected with His oneness with the Father's mind—with His obedience—with His saying, 'I delight to do Thy will,'—with His 'not my will but Thine be done,'—with His full entrance into the purposes of grace by which God was to be glorified in the salvation of man.

When we think of that glory, and that it consists of redemption, is it any wonder that the Redeemer, should be found in glorified human nature in heaven?

We can well believe that this contrast will be recognized by the Father also. His rejoicing is in the Son—it is on the Son He looks with infinite complacency—the Son's interests are His; and we can well believe that the Father rejoices in the contrast between the feet like unto fine brass as if they burned in a furnace, now that redemption is accomplished, and those feet weary and pierced while it was being wrought out.

A contrast will be presented to the Father's eye throughout eternity by those who have been redeemed by the Son, and who are one with Him—who according to their capacity shine after His image in glory. But how different the contrast which *they* present and that which is shown by Jesus. He has come to His glory through sinless sorrow, and travail, and pain—they through that which was full of sin. Christ's robe was never stained, ours can only be white as washed in His blood. This, however, will not hinder God's glory in our contrast, nor our own joy. The death of Christ involved it, purchased it; we shall throughout eternity acknowledge it. We, who have been sinners, shall in our light reflect the glory of Him who died for sin.

Let this prospect cheer us now. Let us look forward with great longing and assurance to that time when we also, no longer in depressed but in glorified manhood, shall be with the One who now has the headship of humanity in glory. Yes! let such a light as this cheer us in our sorrow, make us content when we are passed over, enrich us in our seasons of poverty, and raise us when we are depressed. We are not always to have dusty and toil worn feet; we are not always to be amid the depressions and sin veilings of a clouded humanity —there was joy set before Jesus, and in the power of it He endured His cross, and despised its shame —there is joy set before us, and let us try and do something in the power of it after the example of our Lord.

Oh, yes! often let us look upward, often onward —often away from the present gloom to the future light, and the present unrest to the future peace. It is partly for this purpose that the future is unveiled in any degree—it is meant to be a power in the spiritual life. And there is no sphere so lowly but that it may enter into it.

Poor toiling men and women engaged in the meanest occupations may raise their eyes from the midst of them, and look at the glorified Saviour, and at His feet shining like fine brass. He was revealed to St. John, not for himself alone but for us—the eye of the apostle saw for the universal church. Let us distinctly refuse to allow any earthly occupation, if our lawful one, to degrade us by pinning us down to the dust amid which we must walk and work. This is an animating sight, and introduced into the common affairs of daily life may enable us to do our work in them amid the shining of heaven's own light.

Let us next note the fulness of this revelation—it shews us Christ from head to foot—from the head and the hairs white like wool, as white as snow, down to these feet like unto fine brass, as if they burned in a furnace.

This, then, is the manifestation in glory of a *whole* Christ. It might seem at first sight that we should not need any exhortation, to avail ourselves of the privilege of contemplating a whole and full Christ. But in truth we do.

We are so one-sided—so narrow-minded—so apt to fix upon parts without their relation to the whole, (and thus, so apt to violate or to miss the harmonies of truth,) that we need to be reminded that even of Jesus, a part is not the whole; and that no one part of His character or beauty was intended to satisfy our souls.

Many of our mistakes in the Christian life come from partial views of Christ, from missing the harmony, symmetry, and perfect proportion of His character. That mistake never can be made in glory.

Here you find one Christian fixing on His humility, another on His zeal, another on His holiness, another on His unworldliness, and so on; and perhaps bending all their energies to attainment in that particular grace by which they have been so much struck; and while doing so, other beauties of Jesus are unperceived, and so uncopied.

Now, here is Christ with God in heaven—and we see how He is with His Father, and how He is viewed by Him, viz., in harmonious entirety.

In Daniel's image the head was resplendent of fine gold, but the body passed through a series of deteriorations, until at length the feet were only a mixture of iron and clay. Here, where all human might was combined, and the image presented was that of earthly dominion and beauty at its best, gradual failure is what we see—the perfection of the head was not sustained—the feet were not perfect even after their kind; with the iron was a mingling of clay.

The want of sustainment is a leading characteristic of all earthly excellence. We find it in ourselves—whatever we may have attained to, there is always a tendency to deteriorate.

But the man Christ Jesus was above this want. His was in its fulness, that "path of the just which shineth more and more unto the perfect day." The head was glorious, and the feet too—there was perfection in carrying out thought into action—

harmony between the thoughts of the head, and the actings of the hands, and the walkings of the feet.

And let this thought weigh with us now; it is full both of comfort and instruction—of comfort, because we see we have to do with a Christ who does not content Himself with simply good intentions. He thought much of His disciples on earth, and then said, "I go to prepare a place for you." With Him action was the natural consequence of thought. And so, we have not to do with a Christ of mere intentions. We shall find His doings equal to His thinkings. And if we do so here, where we must live amid cloudings and drawbacks of many kinds, and where the actings of Christ are to a great extent His helping us amid hindrances, how much more shall it be the case in that land where hindrances are done with for ever. Then we shall see what it is to have an acting Christ—one whose thoughts and deeds go together—one who proves that He loves not in word only, but in deed and in truth.

And from this contemplation of the Lord, it will be instructive to look for a moment to ourselves. May we have grace given to us to be harmonious from head to foot in our Christian life—neither to think without acting, nor to act without thought. Let us not content ourselves with good thoughts without good deeds—the head without the feet. We have often failed in this respect, and so come short of the glory of God; let us look on Christ, let us think of what He will make even these feet of ours by and by, and let us up, and in our daily walk glorify Him with them now.

The thought also comes into our minds—how should we serve a Being thus all holy, all bright—the very feet like fine brass, as though it burned in a furnace. Let us look at that head, and glance downward to those feet, and then think nothing small, nothing to be neglected in our walk and life. Let us try with all holiness to serve—to copy—to be so far as we can worthy of a Being all holy. One writes this with shrinking, for what have we been in the past? what are we now? yea, what can we ever hope to be while in the flesh? but we must not withhold on this account; we must set the pattern before us, and try to become as like it as we can.

The head and the feet are both glorious in light, and so the eye cannot fix upon any part in which there is imperfection or short-coming in the glory of the Lord—any part in which there can be the least sympathy with evil; but we need not be discouraged on that account. Though He has no sympathy with sin, He has with the poor sinner—He knows our frame, He took experience of our temptations, He is well aware that we are open to attack from head to foot, and that we are weak all over, and that our feet are set in slippery places;

and He who has feet like unto fine brass as though it burned in a furnace, will hold up our feet as they travel Zionwards, until at last He sets them down upon the land where there are none to hurt or destroy, and where there is the rest which now "remaineth for the people of God."

Another blessed thought suggested to us by this mention of Christ from head to foot in glory is this. The saints shall see, and shall rejoice in a whole Christ in heaven.

Such a view we have not now. We seem unable to take in much about the Lord at once. And in consequence our joy is not full. It may be great in one contemplation and another of the Lord, but it is not full. In heaven we shall rejoice in everything belonging to Christ. All His character will be presented to us in its variety of beauty; and if we know what it is to feel joy at the realization of any one of His manifestations of Himself here, how much more shall we feel it when He dwells with us in full gracious manifestation of Himself there.

Then shall His people know how wholly He was theirs in the past; they shall do so, by feeling how wholly He is theirs now. Yes! that is the way we shall read our past—all the patience, and tenderness, and righteous and loving dealing of it. We shall know much of our own histories then, and they will be full of Christ. We shall wonder then at the greatness of the gift of God in giving us a *whole* Christ, and that, when we were in a world and a body of sin.

We could not enjoy a whole Christ when we were thus circumstanced, because the flesh was ever pulling us down to a low standard, and entering into conflict with this and that which was glorious in Jesus; but now all these impediments are removed, the head, the girded form, the feet, the hands, all are ours, even as all *of us* is His.

And that will satisfy the longings of intensest love. Intense absorbing love does not willingly lose anything of the one that is loved; it craves the ministry of the head, and hand, and foot; of thought, and deed. We could no more do without the feet of Jesus in glory, than we could without His head; without the instruments and symbols of His long travel, than that of His thought on our behalf. We should say, "Where are the feet which were weary, which were pierced, which accepted the sacrifice of a woman's love, at which the afflicted were cast and made whole?" We shall not have so great a loss as this missing of the feet of Christ. The Father has given Him unto us a whole Christ; as a whole Christ He offered Himself on Calvary; as a whole Christ He is our representative and sacrifice now, saying on our behalf, "They pierced my hands and my feet;" and less than a whole Christ we could not do with in heaven.

The feet of Jesus may well be taken to represent all that was most lowly. The unloosing of the shoe latchet—the covering of the foot was the humblest task which John the Baptist could represent himself as doing for Jesus; and when the Lord Himself would stoop to the lowest act of service, and teach His disciples to do the same, the washing of feet was the one He chose. That His own feet should now be thus gloriously exalted in heaven is not without some teaching for us in this direction.

We find, then, that which was most lowly on earth exalted in heaven, and that with intensity of brightness. The feet are sharers with the head, they occupy a position of association.

No doubt Jesus during His earthly walk saw all lowly deeds in their true present and future dignity. He knew how and why it was that He who would be greatest must be the servant of all. He connected service and reward together. And in His mind all lowly deeds associated themselves with high thoughts; they were invested with a dignity wherewith His knowledge of the mind of the Father enabled Him to clothe them.

And it is just here that we fail. We have little power of association; we isolate things and deeds from principles and thoughts, and then the things become burdensome, and the duties toil, and failure is too often the result.

Jesus never did a lowly deed, or took up a lowly position, or uttered a lowly speech, without a consciousness of the true nobility attached to them. By the very fact of their lowliness they had other world connections; they linked themselves with the head and the hair white like wool, with the girding of the golden girdle, with the eyes as a flame of fire, and the feet like unto fine brass, as though they burned in a furnace. With what joy, with what power did Jesus perform these deeds under these conditions! He was always dealing with what had been kindred to glory—association with heaven—oneness with His Father—connection with His own future high position.

Let us try to bring all lowliness into association. Let us try and see the capacities of expansion which exist in lowly deeds. They are like little seeds which can produce something very unlike themselves; let us think not only what they appear on earth, but what they really are in heaven; aye, and what they will be by and by, when the full time for development shall have come.

No one can get a right idea of a thing by looking only at a part of it; we certainly do not get a right idea of the blessedness of lowly deeds, thoughts, or ways, by going no farther than this life.

Let us bind heaven and all of heaven to our humble duties and walks on earth; let us look at our Great Head and see the glory which is now His; let us believe that in our measure and according to our capacity so shall it be with us.

What could be more humble than a little child, but He presented such in a position of dignity, saying, "Of such is the kingdom of heaven." The kingdom of heaven! in its bright eternal meaning let it touch and gild all the service of earth—let the light from the feet of brass shine upon us, as well as that from the eyes which are as a flame of fire; let us remember that He who stands thus glorious, His earthly service all ended, once said, 'I am among you as He that serveth.'

Let us set about the ennobling of our service, of our humble places, and positions, and opportunities at once. We have only to take the nobility which God has already attached to them, and it is done. Let us not call anything mean or common, or unclean, if it be the way in which we are to serve God. Let us be afraid of no soiling save that of sin. Mud and dust there are in plenty here; and few steps can we take without encountering and perhaps being troubled with the one or the other; but that is the very service out of which will come the brightness of the future, and the rest of the people of God.

Life, and common every day service, and duties, will wear a new aspect to us, when we see them tending to such a glorious consummation, and we shall have fresh heart and spirit for our work. We shall be more content with humble things, and more willing to bear the misjudgings of the world; and we shall take up many a sphere which otherwise would have been left unfilled. The future will compensate abundantly for the present, and we shall both do, and bear, for a joy which is set before us.

The lowly ministries and ministers of God we shall exalt and not despise; and we shall see in many a washer of feet one who himself shall hereafter stand with glorious feet in heaven.

Thus much, then, from the bare fact of having a mention made of the feet of Jesus in heaven— that which is lowliest of man in the very abode of God. May the feet which went about doing good during the Lord's sojourn on earth, still minister to us from the height of glory—so that abiding in Him, we may walk even as He walked, and at last be with Him where He is.

The head and the feet are both glorious in light, all glory, all light in Christ Jesus.

And so we see the impossibility of fixing on any imperfect part in Christ which can sympathize with evil.

This is one of the great differences between Him and the greatest characters on earth. The purest and the best here have some sympathies, however small, with evil. None of them can say as Jesus did, 'the Prince of this world cometh and hath nothing in me.' We may not be aware ourselves that this sin and shortcoming, or excess whatever it may be in which the sin consists, comes not merely from a temptation, but from our inward sympathy with evil; but were it not for that measure of sympathy, the temptation could do nothing. Then Jesus was triumphant, sin found no sympathy in Him. Neither in the thought of the head, nor the affection of the heart, nor the way of the feet, did it find seed-ground on which it could sprout.

There are two thoughts in connection with this which concern us much. One is, we must take a whole Christ; the other, we must will Christ to take the whole of us.

Many men have part Christs. What they have is true as far as it goes; but it is only a whole Christ that can save us, or that can lift up our moral natures. Therefore let us dwell in our minds on all of Jesus; let us think of what He was, and what He felt, and what He did, and how He did it; and what He would not do, and how and why He left it undone—of Jesus in this relationship, and that, everything that we can learn about Him, in every way. He exists as 'the man' Christ Jesus. He is in glory as the man Christ Jesus, not only for Himself, but for us; the soul that has any adequate conception of what Jesus is, knows as the bride says in Canticles, that He is altogether lovely, and therefore altogether to be desired.

Moreover: we must will—nay, if we think thus of Christ, we cannot help thus willing that He should take the whole of us. Our desire will be the whole of Him for us, and the whole of us for Him. We could not so to speak fit a whole Christ to ourselves, unless our whole selves were given to Him.

No doubt many of our spiritual sorrows, and some of the fretfulness of our spiritual life come from the leaving out (not perhaps designedly) of some part of the whole self. We have that to which Christ is not fitted; and that to which Christ is not fitted is unsavoury, and unsanctified, and troubles the fineness of our spiritual sense, and disturbs the balance of a perfectly healthy spiritual constitution. The sanctification of the whole body and soul is accomplished by the fitting to us a whole Christ—it is in a whole Christ that we shall be presented without spot or blemish or any such thing.

There are, it may be quite unconsciously on our part, some withholdings, be they more or less, in all of us, from Christ; something to which we do not want Him to fit His whole self. Out of these withholdings come weakness, and sin, and sorrow. And so it will be well for us often to speak to Christ on this matter;—to say, 'O my Saviour take me altogether. I want to be wholly thine. Thou hast purchased me altogether; Thou didst give Thy whole self for my whole self, therefore it is all Thine, and as Thine take it.'

This will be fully after God's mind, for His way of raising us is not by contenting Himself with us as imperfect, but by bringing us into connection with One who is perfect, by placing a perfect ideal before us.

We often seek to attain our end by lowering the standard to accommodate the weak; God never lowers His standard but He gives strength whereby that standard may be reached.

And here the ideal which God puts before us is a real one also. It has the immense advantage of being the actual; not the dream of a poet, or the symmetrical figure of the painter, but a life of fact.

We are not then to lose ourselves in any of our contemplations of our Lord, His life, His death, His present life in glory, His very self are all to be living realities to us. The present life in glory is ours, just as much as was the life of suffering, and the death of shame. Let us look upon the feet burning like fine brass in the light of as solid a reality for us, as those same feet when sitting wearily at Sychar, or hanging pierced on Calvary.

We do not rejoice as we ought at the perfection of Christ's holiness, we do not admire it as we should, viz., with a consciousness of self-interest therein.

The thought of His holiness ought not to affright us; what He has He gives to us; it should be a source of gladness. I admire it in Him, and He says, 'What is mine I give to thee.'

For from this presentation of the feet I assume that Jesus is here wholly in the aspect of glorified manhood—the Son of God, and God—but presented in His being of manhood for us; and all that He has in manhood He has for His people—therefore the light and glory of His feet—of His holy ways, of His completeness is mine, if I can only realize it. That *head*, and those *eyes*, are wonderful, but not more so to me, nor are they of deeper concern to me than these "*feet* like unto fine brass, as if they burned in a furnace."

CHAPTER XVI.

THE FEET OF JESUS THE PLACE OF MANIFESTED POWER.

"*And his feet like unto fine brass, as if they burned in a furnace.*"—Rev. i, 15.

THERE never was a greater mistake made with regard to our blessed Lord, whether considered in his life of humiliation on earth, or of glory in heaven, than to think of him as One whose loving-kindness had anything in it akin to weakness. The balance of His character forbade that.

We seldom possess a specific virtue in any striking degree without its filching from something else; very often it is not anything positive in itself, but rather a negation of something else.

And judging of Christ after our own imperfect standard, we not unfrequently exalt some one of His perfections at the expense of another.

Now here Jesus is represented as One standing in great strength. His feet are like unto fine brass. There is no yielding, no element of weakness here—nothing for mere maudlin sentiment to indulge in.

And this strength had a twofold relation—one to us and one to Satan; and towards each it is put forth.

And first as regards ourselves.

Now when we think of Christ, it is generally only in our relation to sin, viz., as our Saviour from its curse. It is to be feared that many of us think little comparatively of His being to us a Saviour from its power. Even of His sufferings in our behalf, how much more we think of the physical than of the mental part. We are melted at the thought of the buffetings, and spittings, and scorn, of the blood flowing from the wounds; we smite our breasts and say: 'Woe is me, that I was the cause of all this,' but we think little of the mental anguish—of the meaning of 'My God, my God, why hast Thou forsaken me?'—of the loading down of the guilt of a world's sin on Him who was of purer eyes than to behold iniquity, on Him who shrank in horror from even its slightest stain.

It is indeed well that our ideas of Christ's strength should associate themselves with immense power to love, immense to save, immense to help, but all is inharmonious, incomplete, unless we see that strength in His manifested holiness also.

The way to slay sin in our daily life is to live day by day with a holy Saviour—to feel that our closest contact is with one who cannot bear sin—to realize that we are living in the presence of One, whose ordinary manifestation of Himself is one of strength in holiness.

Effort in the spiritual life is good, but it is doubtful whether we do not in some degree take wrong views about it. We think more of holiness by effort, than holiness by habit. The latter is what is presented to us in the feet burning like fine brass. There Christ stands in the calmness of strength and light; and He would have the power and glory of His position operate on us.

We shall never know the power of Jesus if we look only at His cross, and forbear the looking at Himself. His cross was only of avail because of what He was. If we have accepted it, we may pass beyond its violence into the calm of His present life, and draw strength for our spiritual life, not only from Christ's death for sin, but from His life in holiness; each day may be spent in the presence of the calm, brilliant power of the Holy One—"the feet like unto fine brass" being practically put with heavy tread on our rising sin—the manifested holiness of Jesus acting on us and for us with great strength.

We must conquer sin, not only by negative, but by positive means—not only by our view of Christ's death, but of His life. God meant us to go on from the cross when it had done its work, to live with a living Christ—yes, we are privileged not only laboriously to find out how holy He was in this and that acting in life, but to look at Him as now fully revealed in the holy place itself.

This sight will do wonders for us in our seekings

after a holy life. We shall have all the power and spring which belong to companionship with the living—all the mighty influence which belongs to example—all that appertains to a presence. We shall take heed to our ways when we think of the feet like unto fine brass—to where we set our feet, when we think of *His* feet.

And when sin rises up like a wreathing snake, and, perhaps ere we know anything about it, has risen so high that we cannot put our foot upon it, then are we not without help—then let us call to mind the feet of brass—their exaltation, their vantage ground, their strength, their purity; and they shall crush the head of the monster we dread, and we shall escape.

Let us in imagination lay the filthy thing beside the feet like unto fine brass, as if they burned in a furnace—and many a dark temptation, when thus exposed by that light, shall perish by the development of its own vileness; but if it should still put forth its strength, we may invoke the power of the feet to crush it—and they will.

Let us not be afraid of the holiness of these feet —or think that we do them wrong by asking that they may come into contact with, and stamp upon our sin. His feet—even as His hands, and head, and all points of His humanity—are for us; there is nothing in the human form, or human mind, or exalted human position of Jesus, which does not fit into something human belonging to us. We may look at all and each, and say, 'What is this, and this, and this, to me?'

There are some beautiful words of Edward Irving on Christ's retention of His own holiness, while He deals with unholiness, which may encourage us. For though they speak principally of the treading down of Satan, still they apply as well to the treading down of that Evil One in us, when we invoke Christ's aid that this should be done.

"After the same manner do I interpret the second symbol by which our Bishop is set forth, 'His feet like fine brass.' The word translated, 'fine brass,' is one to interpret which aright hath puzzled the learned. It is composed of two words; the one, the common word for brass, and the other derived from a root which signifies to flow, or to be liquid, or to melt. The true meaning of the word, therefore, would be brass made liquid, or melted. Now, we find that the laver and his foot (Ex. xxxviii, 8), in which the priests washed themselves, was made of the looking glasses of the women which assembled at the door of the tabernacle of the congregation. Working upon this idea, it is a discovery not many years old, that if you take the finest brass, such as mirrors were wont to be made of, and cast it into the furnace, you produce another kind of brass, which shall take on no rust, nor tarnish from exposure to water or weather of any kind. Of this the laver and his foot were made, to the end that, though filled with water, and even exposed to the action of the air, they might never tarnish. And of this brass melted over again I believe our Lord's feet are represented to be in the passage before us, and because it is never tarnished, it is, as I think, said, that His feet are like unto melted brass, as if they burned in a furnace.

"Now, what is the meaning of the symbol thus explained?

"It is to express His holiness, that when He should come to tread down His enemies, to tread the wicked under His feet, to tread the wine-press of the wrath of God, though He walked amongst defilement, and did tread upon abomination, yet were His feet not tarnished therewith, but remained in their original purity and brightness. This metal (χαλκολιβανου), brass molten, is chosen, because, as now appeareth, it taketh no tarnish from the pollution of the air, nor from the pollution of the earth, nor yet from the pollution of the sea. So, also, His eyes, though they look upon all iniquity, are not polluted therewith; and His feet, though they tread down all iniquity, are not polluted therewith. The fire refineth all things, and is not polluted with them. They come in contact with it, and their impurities are expelled. Their dross is carried off, and the pure metal floweth out in a pure stream.

"So, likewise, these feet of brass trample upon the lion, and the adder, and the young lion, upon the mire and the clay, and the mass of rottenness, upon the devil, upon the grave, upon corruption, but are never defiled by any of them.

"I need never shrink, then, from bringing my sin —the sin I hate, and would flee from, and be rid of, into contact with Christ. For this purpose is the Son of God manifested, that He might destroy the works of the devil—for this purpose manifested to me in glory, that He might destroy my sin. His feet, shining like fine brass, have power against my sin, even as they had when they hung upon the tree. May they have more power, is the cry of every believer. Stand beside me with Thy glorious feet, is the longing of every earnest heart. Oh, where should we be, if Jesus could not stand in the midst of the vilest unholiness without being unholy Himself? He it is who can walk upon coals and not be burned, who can touch pitch and not be defiled; therefore, I may invoke His presence and His power—the brightness and the strength of the feet like unto fine brass against the strength of the darkness of my temptation, or my sin."

On Satan especially will this power be brought to bear.

Antichrist is to be destroyed with the brightness of the coming of the Lord. And as to Satan himself, he was doomed from the beginning to be destroyed by the crushing of these feet. On those feet was the bruised heel—and it was the bruised heel that was to be crusher or bruiser of the serpent's head. There was to be a place of brightness, but it was first to be a place of suffering.

And, in truth, it was thus with Jesus, as it was to be with His church. It is through sorrow we pass to joy, through gloom to light. Our places of suffering shall be places of brightness. There is something very teaching and comforting in the bruising of the heel, and the brightness of the foot. Let us make use of it. Let us connect the very seat of trial with thoughts of joy; if the head be smitten of the Lord, then that head and those hairs are white like wool, as white as snow; and elsewhere we read that on that head were many crowns. The voice that cries, 'My God, my God, why hast Thou forsaken me?' is now as the sound of many waters—the pierced right hand has in it many stars—the visage marred more than that of any of the sons of men, is as the sun shining in its strength; the body first clothed with a mocking purple robe, and then stripped for crucifixion, is clothed with a garment down to the foot, and girt about the paps with a golden girdle. For our weary foot or hand, for our pierced heart, for our aching head, there is an opposite of blessedness and joy for every grief they have respectively endured.

But we are now to speak of the power brought to bear on Satan. It will indeed be a crushing one. The brightness of Jesus is not manifested now in this world of shadow and gloom. Gleams of it are seen here and there, but the day of manifestation has not yet come. But when Jesus shall be revealed, Satan shall be struck down. That evil spirit has come into conflict with power many times, and with power in many forms, but it was always that with the element of human weakness and sin somewhere in it. But when he stands face to face with perfect holiness, it will smite him. He fled from it after the encounter in the wilderness, when Jesus was weak, as regards the flesh, from fasting; how much more will he have to flee when there shall be no reason why Jesus should veil His power in any way—when the time for crushing shall have come.

This will be the triumph of light. The light will drive the prince of darkness back into his own abyss. Not only will he not come to the light because his deeds are evil, but he will flee from it, he will be driven before it. Great are the powers of light in nature, and equally great, yea, greater, in grace; the coming of the One with the feet like unto fine brass as though they burned in a furnace, will be the full sun-rising of which we now have only feeble dawnings here and there.

Let us take courage, then, however great may be the present power of Satan either in the world, or in our own hearts. Let us have all the confidence inspired by the knowledge that we are on the winning side. Let us feel that we are contending with a doomed enemy. Let us hail every glimpse of the dawn of the brightness which shall destroy not only the devil's antichrist, but the devil himself; and let us look forward to the full manifestation of the Sun of Righteousness Himself. It is only by His coming that the night-clouds will be dispelled, and the nations of the earth shall walk in light.

But we need not wait for a long-distant future ere we can receive light ourselves. We, too, must look to the future for full revelation, but Jesus may be brightening to us every day.

And thus our evil shall be consumed. Let us say, ' O, my Saviour, be so bright in my soul that evil shall not be able to live in Thy presence—come with light, ever more light that the evil may appear dark, ever more dark—thus shall Satan be crushed in us, meeting in every believer a foretaste of his final and perfect doom.'

These feet of Jesus are thus shining in the way of final development.

Christ always knew whither and to what He was going; the future always had its power with Him. He looked to the end—He remembered the joy which was set before Him. His Father did not expect Him to go through the world, and His mission in it, without having light before Him. He also had respect unto the recompense of reward.

We may remember that we do not serve God for nought, and that remembrance may exercise its influence on our life. It is God's plan always to set something before us—that we should be people of hope, and reach forth to the object of our hope.

None who looked upon the wayworn feet of Jesus could have known that, wrapped up in those travellings, and wearinesses, and nail-piercings, was the brightness. They were as unlike it as the hard bud is unlike the unfolded flower, gorgeous in colour, and sweet in its scent. But they were the germs which were to develop. Only they must develop in the proper time and way. Christ could not hurry the development of His own life into its eventual glory. Its bud, like all other buds, must unfold, it must not be picked to pieces. And so He passed through all His trials—He spent long years before He came out into ministry at all; He rejected the premature glory of sovereignty which men would have thrust upon Him; He did not judge the world, for His time of judgment had not yet come.

To many the present might have seemed to be thrown away, to be all lost time; nothing to all human appearance was coming of it; but the future was maturing—that future of which in this passage we have a glimpse.

The present always has its use; it is never lost, never being thrown away, unless we will it to be so. Let us look at it in this light—ever saying, 'This, and this, and this is an unfolding.'

Alas! what a fearful unfolding lies before many —to what a final development are they going!

They will be landed by a natural process in a terrible future!

And now a word or two upon Christ's ability to bring light with Him. He has light in Himself, and light for us.

Jesus walked in light Himself while He was upon the earth, though men did not see that such was His path—His was that path of the just which shineth more and more unto the perfect day. "In Him was life, and the life was the light of men, and the light shineth in darkness, and the darkness comprehended it not."

But what could not be revealed on earth, is revealed in heaven—we are allowed to see what the feet and path of Jesus really are.

In all Christ's comings to us now, in all His ways with us, in all His leadings into duties, He comes with feet all light and bright. The duties and dispensations may seem dark, but if He be with us, His feet will bring light into them. The light will come in its own time. Jesus does not change dispensations—sorrow remains sorrow; but He comes with his own light into them, and then the sorrow remains a sorrow, and yet is turned into joy.

Let us believe, then, in Christ's ability to bring light into all darkness. Let us seek to see the feet, and all will be well; let our anxiety be, not lest we should fall into any trouble; but lest if we do, Jesus should not be in it.

There lies before me a place of shadows—the valley of the shadow of death. That valley I cannot enter without Christ. But with Him, even of that place I may say, "Yea, though I walk through the valley of the shadow of death, I will fear no evil, for Thou art with me, Thy rod and Thy staff they comfort me."

The feet of light are what I hope for there—the feet light, and the footfalls on before me light also, so that I need not be afraid. I shall know that they are the once-pierced feet, and, therefore, they are mine—they are the feet which lay in the grave, and are now all glorious, and all for me, coupling the darkness of the tomb with the radiance which lies beyond.

CHAPTER XVII.

THE FEET OF JESUS THE PLACE OF STRENGTH.

"*And when I saw him, I fell at his feet as dead.*"
—Rev. i, 17.

WE commenced this volume with the consideration of 'many' at the Feet of Jesus, we now conclude it with the consideration of 'one;'—the 'many' were all sorts and conditions of men, who in mind and body were afflicted; the 'one' is the beloved apostle—he who lay in the bosom of his Lord, and who now was in exile for His sake.

We are glad that it should be so—that whether through 'many' or 'one' it should be the same story—all mercy—all love. The cradle was love, the cross was love, the living was love, the death was love—it was all love in this world; and what is more meet, than that we should be presented with a picture of love when the other world is unveiled to us also.

The apostle hearing suddenly behind him the voice of a great trumpet, and seeing the glory of this wonderful Being, is overwhelmed by both sound and sight. He was simply and purely in the flesh; and as such could not stand up in presence of another world's manifestation, to say nothing of its extreme intrinsic majesty and overwhelming glory.

Though it was his beloved Lord, yet it was that Lord in glory; and that glory produced its natural result—the apostle fell at the feet of Christ.

There was no opportunity of reasoning, or of self reassurance; the amazing brilliancy and awfulness of the Being before him precluded that; the apostle fell like one dead. Not even at the feet could he have recovered strength if left to himself —for, as we have just seen, they were flashing with light and glory. They could not be held or embraced as in the times of Christ's flesh, or even of that body, of whatsoever nature it was, in which he lived for awhile on earth between the resurrection and ascension; and now, even they, though only *the feet* of Jesus, with their furnace-like glory were enough to scorch the stoutest heart.

Under these, as under all circumstances of difficulty and distress, the relief comes from Christ Himself; and from Christ, by the manifestation of Himself. He speaks to the beloved apostle, reassures and comforts him by touch and word, saying:—"Fear not, I am the first and the last; I am He that liveth and was dead, and behold I am alive for evermore, and have the keys of hell and death;" or more correctly "I am the first and the

The Place of Strength.

last,—the Living One, and I became dead, and behold I am alive for evermore," &c.

Let us place in the following order the few thoughts which the nature and design of this volume suggest on this the last appearance in scripture of the Feet of Jesus. I. The apostle fallen as dead at the feet. II. The apostle not allowed to remain as dead; and III. The apostle, how aroused from that death state, and comforted.

I. The position of John at the feet of his glorified Lord is that of one as dead. Let us keep clearly before our minds that John, though the beloved apostle, was still simply a poor mortal in flesh and blood; and as such, had no inherent power to stand up beneath any spiritual manifestation, much less under such an overwhelming blaze of glory as that which he now saw. No doubt there will be abundant strength for sustaining such manifestations hereafter, but unless there be special strengthening, not now. John was conscious that he was flesh and blood, with all its sinfulness, and physical nervousness; and his acting was exactly conformable to the circumstances in which he found himself. When Paul had that wonderful vision, and heard sounds which it was not lawful for a man to utter, he had some suitability of nature given to him at the time, and for the time; for whether he was in the body or out of the body he could not tell; but John knew well enough that he was in the body, and that without

x

any preparation of any kind he had seen the Lord in His glory.

Such were the natural effects of the vision of the Lord; and we may pause for a moment to ask what will be its effect on the wicked, when the days of the purposes of mercy are ended, and the only revelation of Jesus will be for judgment? It is a fearful thought. He will be able to destroy with the brightness of His appearing. When every eye shall see Him, and they also who pierced Him; what will be their sensations, when they look upon this body, as that which they bruised, pierced, insulted, scoffed, spat upon, and despised. For all such fearful deeds are laid to the account of the rejectors of the Lord; and now must they reckon concerning them with Him, as in this body of glory.

And touching this body of glory and our sin—the more special, the more glorious the manifestation of Christ to us; the more must it ever, from its very nature, waken in us a consciousness of our inability in ourselves to stand before Him. We are ever panting after knowing more and more of Christ; and what, if some manifestation like this be sent to us!—if, instead of seeing Him by the well-side weary, or with feet being anointed, or pierced, or manifesting themselves in witnessing love, as to the disciples, we be called upon to behold them burning like brass; and even then, only as parts of a great perfection of glory!

We cannot see aught of His glory and purity without being smitten with a consciousness of our sin—we *must* fall before Him.

We may well tremble at our being only in the flesh; and if left to ourselves might wish never to have any vision of Christ here, beyond what we believe flesh to be capable of bearing.

But Jesus gives revelations from time to time, which the merely human never could bear—which it never was constructed to bear; and for all such revelations He will always give something which is beyond what is merely human in the way of strength. As is thy day so shall thy strength be; as is thy sorrow, as is the immense revelation of the divine majesty and thy demerit, the one infinitely high, the other infinitely low, so shall be thy strengthening and upholding from the Lord.

The practical point which I wish to impress upon the reader is this,—beloved as he may be of the Lord, yea, let me say of *his* Lord—there may come that upon him in his spiritual life, which as a manifestation of his Lord's glory, yea, even of his Lord's love, may be altogether too much for him.

It may be that, the reader's experiences in Christian life have partaken more of the character of gloom than brightness; and that what he fears for the time to come is overwhelming from that source. Well, the same observation holds good for him. This dead and overwhelmed state is not one in which it is the mind of Christ that any man should stay. Saul of Tarsus fallen to the ground must not remain there. It may be necessary that we should fall to the ground—that we should with the fulness of our nature acknowledge the height of glory or the depth of sorrow; the very physical frame will faint or weep from the one as well as the other, but falling to the ground and staying there are two very different things. This is taught us in the fact that—

II. The apostle was not allowed to remain as one dead. And so our minds are at once brought back to Jesus again. It is the same Jesus on earth and in glory, shewing kindness to those who by *any* means are brought to His feet.

"By any means"—and so there is great security—security in the immense diversity of experiences of the people of God—of all; from the poor creature who, falling there, says, "God be merciful to me a sinner," up to a beloved apostle, or any disciple, overwhelmed with the majesty of the One he loves. Can we imagine any two persons under more different circumstances than Saul of Tarsus and John of Patmos? The one caught red-handed in murder falls to the ground, and the other, in suffering for the very Lord who appeared, falls likewise. Of neither is it the will of the Holy One that he should lie prostrate; to the trembling and astonished Saul the Lord says 'arise;' and on John lying at

His feet like one dead, He lays His hand and says, 'Fear not.'

Diverse indeed are the acquaintanceships with the feet, made in diverse ways. Every one has its place; and all together they form a great ministry for the Church, for they help to give a more perfect image of Christ.

And now this—the last one with which we are presented in the Scripture—comes in very beautifully. For though of necessity it shews Christ, the One whom we have known, admired, and loved so long in suffering, as brilliant beyond all the power of human sight to bear, still it shews us man lifted up so as to bear it; the very One who overcame by His glory, giving the strength by which the vision of that glory could be borne.

It shews us more than this—even the man thus cast down raised up for lengthened communion with the glorified One. We shall be lifted up to sustain the sight of the glorified One, and to hold communion with Him. We cannot imagine a manifestation of glory being pushed farther than this, or a mortal's being in more need of succour; the succour is given—a witness to us that even poor disciples shall never be allowed to be overborne, no not even by the glory and majesty of their Lord.

The position of the apostle was as that of one dead. It was not the mere fact that he saw a vision of the other world that overwhelmed him.

No doubt, at all times such visions have been too much for flesh and blood. Ezekiel, Daniel, Job's friend, one and all were overcome by such sights; but here it was just the immensity and intensity of the glory which were too much for John.

Perhaps it was needful for our instruction that he should have thus fallen; that the nothingness of the flesh in itself, its want of sustained power even in the most favoured should be proved; that we should learn that when there is about to be most filling, there shall be most emptying first. "Who is sufficient for these things?" was the teaching which John received ere the wonderful visions were unfolded before his eyes.

And now that the apostle lies prostrate at the feet, shining like unto fine brass, as though they burned in a furnace; we ask, 'of what use would it have been to Christ, to the Church, to himself, had he been allowed to remain there?'

That falling had its place, and the apostle rose from the feet of Jesus a deeply self-emptied man, to receive for His Church the fulness of the things He was about to reveal.

No man is intended to occupy a position in the Church which makes him useless. Continued paralysis from fear would be no glory to Christ, no good to man. Every dispensation which comes upon us is not for ourselves alone; the union of the members of the body makes the experience of one to be at least the teaching of all.

The Place of Strength.

So, then—

III. Jesus quickly lays His right hand upon John, the Apostle.

The apostle is raised, not by any coming to of himself, not by any acquired familiarity with the sight which at first overwhelmed him, but by a special and personal act of Christ.

When we cannot reason, being perhaps so overwhelmed as not to be able to say, 'this is my own Lord, therefore He cannot hurt me, He can only do me good;' then we may be sure the Lord Himself will act for us. We may safely leave ourselves in all prospective trials, be they of light or darkness, in His hands. But let us do so with this prayer—"Lord Jesus act out of Thyself. I am willing to have nothing in me; have Thou all in Thyself for me." Thus we shall get rid of the depressions of weakness—of all fears] of the failing of mental powers, yes, even of faith itself. We may come to such a state that sustaining faith will leave us; perhaps intense bodily weakness, perhaps heavy cloudings of Satan will cause this, then we shall be little better than one dead; but the life and the light are in Jesus, and life will act, and light will shine. The right hand conferring fresh life will be laid on us by the One at whose feet we have fallen as dead.

John, then, being utterly self-emptied, and made even like a dead man, is vivified for great and important service. It was with him as with Saul, as with almost if not indeed actually with all; in proportion as God was about to fill him with the revelation of His own things, did He self-empty him—for what self-emptying could go further than the apparent loss of life itself?

But in this, so thoroughly accomplished, no time is lost; the spell is quickly removed, the right hand is laid upon the Apostle, the word of strength is spoken. Jesus says, "Fear not"—then He proceeds to say who He is, and what He will have the Apostle do. "Write," He says to him. It is the Lord's will, not only that the Apostle should live, but that he should do so with comfort and in peace; with an unbroken sense of union with his Lord; with a high capacity for service.

It is indeed no poor slavish life that Christ wills us to lead in presence of His glory. We think too much of the overwhelmings of majesty—we think it the humblest and safest position to lie as dead. But Jesus wills us life, and peace, and usefulness—yes, honour—He lifts us from our own depressions to set us in the liberty of His own high service.

Remember that, dear reader. The enlarging of the heart and the running in the way of the commandments go together. In what sense, then, ask yourselves, are you now engaged—what emptyings have you had—what fillings? Do you know the mind of Christ concerning you, that it is, that fear should vanish, that you should be partakers of the strength of His right hand? "Now know I," said

David in Psalm xx, "that the Lord saveth His anointed, he will hear Him from His holy heaven, with the saving strength of His right hand." That right hand's saving strength is ours—oh, that we may be ever saying with the Psalmist, "Now know I"—"Now know I."

And what a glimpse does this give us of the glory of future service. John was shown here his connection with the glorious One—and was given commission to write for Him—and all that he did was as for the One who had been dead, but was now in light and life. So shall it be hereafter. We shall serve in conscious connection with the glorious One. Here, when we serve Jesus, our service is often undervalued. No one sees Him; the honour of the Master is unknown, and, by consequence, little comes to the servant; and we ourselves are so absorbed in the actual working, or, perhaps, so cast down by the unpleasant surroundings of the work, that, we are but little elevated by the consciousness of the glory of connection with the Lord.

But by and by all service will be done in the power of full consciousness—its honour, and dignity, and glory—its immediate connection with the Lord will be seen and felt.

Meanwhile, let us seek, each of us after our opportunities and according to our commission, to serve. Let us see that Christ wills to be glorified by our life, and not by our death—by our freedom, and not by our fear. The Son sets us free, oh! may we feel that we are free indeed. However it may have been with us in time past, may we henceforth be privileged to look upon our glorified Lord with the consciousness of being in union with Him, and of being partakers of His strength. But should we be overwhelmed by the greatness of the evil in ourselves, or of the glory in Him, or of both combined—then will He surely deal with us in like grace to that wherewith He dealt with John—who "fell at his feet as dead."

Thus, dear reader, we have travelled together through some of the scenes in which we find the Feet of Jesus, and gathered up some thoughts of teaching therefrom; leaving, I doubt not, far more behind than we have borne away. We say some of the scenes, for there remain two, which as belonging to the future we have not touched upon at all. These are—

Zech. xiv, 4: "AND HIS FEET SHALL STAND IN THAT DAY UPON THE MOUNT OF OLIVES, WHICH IS BEFORE JERUSALEM ON THE EAST," &c.

AND

1 Cor. xv, 25: "FOR HE MUST REIGN, TILL HE HATH PUT ALL ENEMIES UNDER HIS FEET."

As I write these lines a telegram stops my pen, bringing to me the tidings of the death of a near and dear relative. I look at the verse next to the one I have written, and I see that "The last

The Place of Strength. 315

enemy that shall be destroyed is death." I thank God; I bless Him that "the Feet of Jesus" passed through the valley of the shadow of death—and that emerging therefrom they were shown to His disciples on earth—to this Apostle in heaven. I thank Him that the keys of Hades and death are in His hands: not in terror, after what I have read here, but in adoration, and oh, that it were in more devotion and love, I, too, desire to fall at

"THE FEET OF JESUS."

www.ingramcontent.com/pod-product-compliance
Lightning Source LLC
Chambersburg PA
CBHW030731230426
43667CB00007B/668